CYBARIS®
AN INTELLECTUAL PROPERTY
LAW REVIEW

Volume 8   2017   Issue 2

EDITOR-IN-CHIEF
Alissa M. Harrington

EXECUTIVE EDITOR
Trevor Haney

NOTES & COMMENTS EDITORS
John Kuehl   Gregory Gunnerson   Chad Reverman

STAFF

Andrew Auderith	Scott Determan	Cassandra Doran
Rachel Foote	Alexander Gutnik	Anna Harper
Zachary Herman	Delavontay Hill	Joshua Humphrey
Mary Grace Hyland	Taylor Kaspar	Jason Kuchar
Sean Michalski	Brian Moen	Amanda Oliver
Lana Rask	Laura Temme	Sandy Wang
	Maria Torres DeJesus	

FACULTY ADVISOR
Ken Port

2017

Cybaris®, an Intellectual Property Law Review, is published two times per year by the students of the Intellectual Property Institute of Mitchell Hamline School of Law at 875 Summit Avenue, Saint Paul, Minnesota, 55105. Telephone: 651-290-6425. E-mail: eic.cybaris@mitchellhamline.edu

Manuscripts: Cybaris®, an Intellectual Property Law Review, welcomes unsolicited manuscripts. All manuscripts submitted for consideration should be double spaced, with citations placed in footnotes that conform to THE BLUEBOOK: A UNIFORM SYSTEM OF CITATION (20th ed. 2015). Please forward all submissions to the Cybaris® Editorial Office at the address listed above.

Opinions expressed in Cybaris®, an Intellectual Property Law Review, do not necessarily represent the views of the publication, its editors, the Mitchell Hamline School of Law, or any person connected therewith.

CYBARIS®
AN INTELLECTUAL PROPERTY LAW REVIEW

Volume 8 2017 Issue 2

Transcript from 2017 Mitchell Hamline Trade Secret Conference, Cybaris scholar symposium

Trade Secret Enforcement: The Reach of Extraterritoriality and its Alternatives
Panelists:
Rochelle Dreyfuss
Christoph Rademacher
Susy Frankel
Nari Lee
Moderated by Sharon Sandeen 181

Student Articles

How South Korea's Improper Solicitation and Graft Act (Kim Young-ran Act) Can Help Protect US Trade Secrets
Lana Rask 208

Cybersecurity in the Marine Transportation Sector: Protecting Intellectual Property to Keep Our Ports, Facilities, and Vessels Safe from Cyber Threats
Rachel Foote 231

TRADE SECRET ENFORCEMENT: THE REACH OF EXTRATERRITORIALITY AND ITS ALTERNATIVES

PANELISTS: ROCHELLE DREYFUSS, CHRISTOPH RADEMACHER, SUSY FRANKEL, NARI LEE
MODERATED BY: SHARON SANDEEN

I.	INTRODUCTION	181
II.	ROCHELLE DREYFUSS	183
III.	CHRISTOPH RADEMACHER	191
IV.	SUSY FRANKEL	194
V.	NARI LEE	201
VI.	DISCUSSION	204

I. INTRODUCTION

Cybaris Editor-In-Chief Alissa Harrington: Thank you, Professor Sandeen. First off, I want to thank Professor Sandeen for her support as we have gone forward with planning this symposium and helping us to reach out to a very esteemed group of academics so that the Cybaris group can put together this panel.

Cybaris is the Intellectual Property Law Review that is now in its eighth year here at Mitchell Hamline. We, first off, want to say that we will be putting out a special symposium trade secret issue very quickly. It will be appended over the summer when Professor Dreyfuss and her writing partner will be adding a paper on what she's going to present on, today.

Until then, we will have a trade secret symposium issue coming out very soon that will include a transcription of this panel. One very quick thing, I know this is an exciting and very passionate topic for all of you, try not to speak over each other so that our transcribers can tell you apart, I would appreciate very much, as will the future readers. That will be available for download and for purchase this summer.

We also have two great student articles on trade secrets that are going to be in the symposium issue. One on Korean trade secret law, written by Lana Rask who is sitting up here at the front table, and one on maritime law and trade secret law, which is actually written by one of our brilliant hybrid students, Rachel Foote.

With that, I'll move on to introducing our panel, which is entitled, "Trade Secret Enforcement: The Reach of Extraterritoriality and Its Alternatives." As I mentioned, we are very honored to have this panel of guests with us from all over the world.

First, Professor Rochelle Dreyfuss, who is from New York, NYU Law, who is the Pauline Newman Professor of Law, the Co-Director of the Engelberg Center on Innovation Law and Policy, the Co-Director of the Competition, Innovation and Information Law Program, and a special thing to us here at Mitchell Hamline—she was a law clerk to Chief Justice Warren Burger. She can go visit his bust in our library which was named after him.

Moving on to Christoph Rademacher, who is a Professor at Waseda University School of Law in Tokyo. He teaches international business and IP law. He was the first tenured foreign professor at that university; he is also of Counsel at the Tokyo branch of Baker & McKenzie, and a bar member both in New York State, and a Solicitor in the Republic of Ireland.

Next on our panel is Professor Susy Frankel, from the Victoria University of Wellington in New Zealand. She is Chair of the IP and International Trade Section there. She is also the Director of the New Zealand Centre of International Economic Law. She is a Barrister, Solicitor in New Zealand, and a Solicitor in England and Wales.

Finally, on the panel we have Nari Lee who is at the Hanken School of Economics in Finland. She is Professor of IP law, specializing in IP and international trade secrets where she has taught at universities all over Europe and Asia.

With that, I will turn it over to our panel. Thank you.

II. ROCHELLE DREYFUSS

Professor Rochelle Dreyfuss: Thank you very much. I want to particularly thank Sharon for letting me present this. This is absolutely the hardest paper I've ever written. Trade secrecy cases are complicated from an applicable law perspective because often activity is spread around several countries. Information is developed in country A, and is licensed to someone in B from which it's misappropriated; then, it might be used in multiple other places.

Determining whose trade secrecy laws applies presents a real puzzle. That problem is complicated by our international commitments to WTO Agreements, TRIPS Agreement and also changes in ALI's approach to both conflicts and foreign relations.

My co-author and I have yet to take a final position on this, and it's a real favor for me to be allowed to present this to you and hopefully get some input.

I'll start with a little background on why I wrote this paper, or am writing the paper. My interest was initially piqued at a conference where the panel right before mine was discussing a 1337 exclusion order issued in a case called TianRui against ITC, so section 1337—or nicknamed 337—actions asked the ITC to exclude goods from the US market when, among other things, the proprietor engaged in "unfair methods of competition."

In TianRui, information for making the goods was appropriated in China, and the question before the commission was, what law should be used to determine whether the appropriation was unfair, US law or Chinese law? The Commission and later the Federal Circuit applied US law, in part on the theory that it didn't matter which law it applied, because US and Chinese trade secrecy laws are identical.

I thought that raised an interesting question, especially in light of two recent developments. First, the United States has been busy through its trade deals and special 301 reports persuading other governments to enact trade secrecy law, and it wasn't at all clear to me that they were enacting laws that were identical to US laws.

Second, the easy decision to use US law seemed to me to fly in the face of a whole series of recent Supreme Court cases that express concern about the friction between national laws in an interdependent world and which laid down a strong presumption against applying US statutes outside the United States.

So, I thought I'd look to see how different trade secrecy laws across the world really were, and if they were different, then I'd think about whether US law should apply to activity in places where the law had taken a different turn. On that, I invited my colleague, Linda Silberman to join me. Linda knows very little about IP law, but she is a well-known and highly regarded conflict scholar whose written extensively on applicable law. She has also served as an expert witness in many applicable law cases, including for the people trying to recover Madoff money that's been secreted in foreign banks.

On the first point, I quickly came to the conclusion that trade secrecy laws are quite different. True that in WTO countries, they are all based on the requirement of Article 39 of the TRIPS Agreement, but Article 39 is fairly bare-boned. The Uniform Trade Secrets Act has not led to uniform trade laws, as we all know. Jim Pooley calls it, "the non-uniform trade secrets act," and the UTSA includes considerably more detail of Article 39 of the Trips Agreement.

The EU just enacted a Directive which Sharon has analyzed extensively; I wish her article had been out since I started this. To hit the high points on the differences I found among national laws, they include things like what counts as a trade secret, things not to try, are protectable? What source of efforts to maintain them are considered reasonable? Do you need to give actual notice to employees? The effect of reverse engineering? What if the information could be reverse engineered? How the defendant acquired it? When is it TP liable? What are the defenses? How long does an injunction last? How do you calculate monetary damages?

These differences aren't surprising. As a normative matter, the value of trade secrets is indeterminate. Some jurisdictions think of trade secrets as an important adjunct to patent law, because the availability of protection encourages research and development of inventions that either aren't patentable or of questionable patentability.

Some jurisdictions think the availability of protection channels people out of the patent war regime and keeps it in a place where knowledge is hidden and can't be built upon by others. That sharing and employee mobility are important to knowledge development, and trade secrecy law interferes with that. Some jurisdictions take a hard line on appropriation, others are more protective of the public domain.

Indeed, in a case after TianRui, a case now captioned, "Sino Legend Against ITC," the differences were apparent. There, too, information was appropriated in China, but the situation was different from TianRui because the trade secrecy action was initially filed in China and the alleged trade secrecy holder lost. Nonetheless, the Federal Circuit applied US law, simply citing TianRui. The Chinese government intervened in that action, objecting to the application of US law to activity on its territory. The Federal Circuit simply ignored it, and the Supreme Court denied cert.

Yet there does seem to be a problem. In its earliest years, the Supreme Court worked with the presumption that US law did not apply extraterritorially; but by the late 20th Century, it had eased up. The culmination was a case called Hartford Fire against California, a 1993 anti-trust case where a conspiracy occurred in the United Kingdom, but the Supreme Court affirmed the application of US anti-trust law because the effect was to restrain trade in the United States.

Significantly, the UK fought back rather than allow US plaintiffs to make off with treble damages, it enacted the Fallback Statute that forbade recovery of those awards. I suspect it was this episode that led the Supreme Court to become concerned about international discord, about friction arising from the extraterratorial application of US law.

In a series of cases, Title VII, other anti-trust laws, the Patent Act, the Securities Act, the Alien Tort Act, civil RICO laws, the racketeering influence corrupt organization, the court pulled back. In Microsoft and Kilbo,** it cautioned that US law does not rule the world. To ensure that national laws were to terminate, the Court revived the presumption, and now defers to Congress. Unless Congress clearly indicates that US interests are so strong, it will chance discord, a law applies only domestically.

To be sure, when the Federal Circuit applied US law in TianRui, it cited some of these cases, but the analysis was confusing and triggered a strong dissent from Judge Moore who noted, "The potential breadth of this holding is staggering. Suppose that goods were produced by workers who operate under conditions that would not meet the United States' labor laws, or workers that would not be paid minimum wage. Would we consider those laws unfair trade practices? Absent clear intent by Congress to apply the law in an extraterratorial manner, I simply cannot believe we have the right to determine what business practices conducted entirely abroad are unfair."

So, our initial research question was on the application of US law, 337 actions, what worked—the GTSA was passed. It adds a civil action to the criminal EEA, of 1996, which was what I just told you, which had a provision on extraterratoriality. We decided to look at that, as well.

Our thought was that, in light of the different normative positions a country could take on trade secrecy, this was an area there was quite a strong potential for discord. What did we decide? We started with the general rule on extraterratoriality that emerges from the recent line of cases—the Morrison Two-Step.

Step one, is there express congressional intent to apply the law extraterratorially? If not, go to step two: characterize the focus of the statute. If the object of the statute's solicitude is US activity, then the application is not considered extraterritorial.

Finally, this case suggests that before the court actually applies the law, it engage in a comedy analysis; even if the statute would seem to apply, the court must nonetheless determine, under the facts of that particular case and in light of the potential remedy, whether it should refrain from applying US law out of respect for other jurisdictions.

How does this all affect trade secrecy cases? The picture in IP is a little complicated because the first modern case on extraterritoriality was Steele against Bulova from 1952. In that case, the Supreme Court applied US trademark law to bar use of the Bulova mark in Mexico. According to the court, acts committed abroad legally lose that character when they become part of an unlawful scheme.

What about congressional intent? The court found in the definitional section of the statute which referenced commerce within the control of Congress. So, it's no surprise that TianRui would reason that US law could be used in 337 actions, which after all, are about goods coming in from abroad, and arguably in unlawful scheme. But, there's a problem. The recent cases on extraterritoriality have held that rote references to the Commerce Clause, or to find commerce are not sufficient to signal intent. They're really a statement about Congress's power to legislate. As some of you may remember, that it was very doubtful that there was federal power to enact trademark legislation under the copyright clause, and Congress put this statement in the second time around.

Because this states Congress's intentions regarding its source of power, such language is generally considered insufficient to overcome a presumption against extraterritoriality. Furthermore, if one looks closely at Bulova, sees careful attention to the comedy factors; the defendant would be a US citizen, watches had flowed back into the United States so there were confused consumers. Mexico had cancelled the defendant's Mexican mark, so the possibility of friction was minimized.

Later cases applying Bulova similar are recently Trader Joe's against Halal where the Ninth Circuit listed a whole bunch of factors on why it would be okay to apply trademark law to use in Canada.

Even the seminal case, Bulova, did not give courts carte blanche to apply US law. Besides that, one of the recent cases in the extraterritoriality line is Microsoft, a patent case. That's the one that warned that US law does not rule the world. There the court wanted a much clearer statement of congressional intent.

The case involved sending software from inside the United States to outside the United States for combination into a computer. It looked like section 271 of the Patent Act deals with that exact issue. Nonetheless, the Supreme held that intent was not expressed enough. A recent case this term Life Sciences against Promega is similar.

Now perhaps different areas of IP are to be treated differently. The trade secrecy cases seem to us more like patent cases than trademark cases, so we think the stricter Microsoft standard applies, or that comedy factors need to be taken more seriously.

How does this all apply to 337 and the DTSA? The 337 actions, a persuasive case can be made that at step one, the presumption is overcome; after all, the entire 337 scheme is about goods coming in from abroad, so it must cover some activity that happened outside the United States. Besides, the remedy is limited to exclusion from the US market, the 337 doesn't rule the world in the sense, and by its terms, it doesn't require or prohibit conduct that takes place abroad.

Even so, the result is uncertain. Consider the next section of 337; that provision was enacted after a court refused to exclude patented goods made abroad on the ground that US patent law doesn't apply outside the United States. After that case, Congress revised the statute so it's now explicitly clear that it covers products made abroad by a process that would infringe a US patent if it had happened here.

In other words, Congress knows how to direct a statute with explicit extraterritorial effect. That it did this for patents and not for trade secrets suggests that only when information is misappropriated in the United States are the goods excludable.

It's also worth nothing that, although exclusions about the US market, the US market is very large. The threat of exclusion can affect behavior elsewhere, so in a sense US trade secrecy law does rule the world under TianRui.

In short, it's possible to say that under step one, 337 was meant to apply US law and determine the unfairness or fairness of foreign conduct, but it's not an entirely persuasive argument. What about step two? Here, one can easily say that the focus of the statute is on an injury to US business and that the object of the statute's solicitude is what Linda and I term, "US trade secrets."

As long as the stolen information is a US trade secret, the statute can be regarded as domestic and, therefore, not within the presumption at all. Note, however, that limiting the statute to US trade secrets raises a different problem. Does it apply only to the trade secrets of US firms? Is that what's meant by, "injury to an industry in the United States?" That sounds fine from the standpoint of applicable law, but it could run afoul of the nondiscrimination provisions of the TRIPS Agreement. I'll come back to that in a minute.

For now, let's go on to the DTSA. The basic provision references commerce, but again that has not been held sufficient in other cases to overcome a presumption against extraterritoriality. To be sure, there is this explicit provision on extraterritoriality; the provision says that it applies to this chapter and the civil remedy is in this chapter, so that looks pretty explicit.

Still, there's a question: When Congress originally enacted this provision, it was a criminal statute. The civil DSTSA inherited the provision. In the Nabisco case, the last one in the series, the civil criminal distinction was critical. In that case the EU brought a civil RICO action to recover for injuries caused by Nabisco's activities, the alleged smuggling of cigarettes which deprived the EU of tax revenue.

RICO, like the EEA, is a criminal statute with a civil provision tacked on. Like the EEA, the criminal statute clearly applies extraterritorially, but the Nabisco court held that the extraterritoriality part of it did not carry over to the civil side. Without a check in the form of prosecutorial discretion, international friction, the court said, is a major concern.

The DTSA similarly lacks a prosecutorial check. More important, the reach of a criminal statute is very different from a civil action. For crimes, there's no such thing as long arm jurisdiction or enforcements against the assets in the United States; instead, the body of the defendant has to be here.

Extradition is possible, but that requires a treaty, cooperation from the other country, and it usually requires that the defendant is accused of doing something that the other country would also regard as a crime. So, that's strong protection against friction and discord.

In addition, there's the matter of relief. Criminal penalties like exclusion orders do not directly affect other countries. In contrast, worldwide junctions and monetary damages granted on a worldwide basis do have a direct extraterritorial effect. Again, the argument to satisfying step one is weaker than I first thought.

How about step two? Here, the focus of the statute is not as explicit as for 337, but once again, an argument can be made that the goal is to protect US trade secrets—that is for both 337 and the DTSA, one might say that the US trade secrecy law is intended to encourage research and development in the United States, to create products of interest to Americans, give jobs, training and opportunities to US scientists and other workers.

But, once again, applicable law analysis runs up against the TRIPS Agreement, WTO agreements. True, courts can apply US law if the statute is interpreted as focusing on US industry in this way, but TRIPS requires nondiscrimination among rights holders. Foreign rights holders have to be treated the same as US rights holders, and foreign rights holders have to be treated equivalently to one another.

If 337 actions and the DTSA are read to protect only the secrets of US firms, then they arguably violate the national treatment obligation. Of course, one could interpret these statutes as protecting trade secrets developed in the United States, even by a foreign firm. I worked as a chemist for a Swiss company before I saw the light and went to law school. It provided me with training, salary, opportunities to innovate to the benefit of my countrymen. So, there's no de jure discrimination, but arguably there is de facto discrimination, and here's why.

In a case about the EU's decision to record geographical indications—GIs—to US growers on less favorable terms than EU growers, the argument was made that US residents could be growing private in the EU and get more favorable treatment, and EU residents could be growing crops in the United States and suffer from the less favorable treatment.

On that basis, the WTO panel agreed there was no de jure discrimination. But it held there was de facto discrimination; it reasoned that EU residents are more likely to be making products in the EU, and US residents are more likely to be making products in the US, so the difference in treatment is a feature and design of the system, and that it constituted a violation of national treatment obligation.

To be sure, trade secrets don't map our nationality as close as geographical indications do; GIs are designed to designate a specific place. Trade secrets don't do that, so, actual treatment for US trade secrets or US industry might be okay if those terms are defined broadly. But, it's questionable. On the whole, US science is done by US residents, and foreign science is done by foreigners, so the degree of protectionism may run afoul.

So, Linda and I looked for a new approach. I see it in state law trade secrecy cases. In state law cases, courts never ask themselves the intent of the legislature. At one time, they were mostly applying common law, not legislation, so the issue of legislative intent never arose.

Instead, in transnational cases, courts apply a conflict analysis. At one time for torts, it would have been lex locus delicti, the law of the place where the tort occurred. Later, they looked to the country with the closest relationship of the transaction, or the strongest interest in the case.

So, BP Chemicals against Formosa, a well-known trade secrecy case, it involved secrets stolen in Taiwan. The Third Circuit held that Taiwan law, not New Jersey law, had the stronger interest—that Taiwan had the stronger interest, and whether the information qualified for protection, and whether it had been misappropriated. The Taiwanese law, rather than New Jersey law applied.

In addition, courts hearing strict states' claims generally honored choice of law clauses in contracts. To me, that seems like the right approach for federal cases, as well. The DTSA, for example, could be seen as codifying the common law, and Congress's intent could be interpreted as using a choice of law analysis to determine which law applied.

Arguable, section 1337 could be approached in the same way. The ITC could determine whether the law of the place where the challenging conduct occurred would regard it as unfair, and then issue exclusion orders. TianRui and St. Allegins,** for example, the ITC would then use Chinese law on the question of misappropriation.

Section approach would have many advantages. US law would not then govern the world. Those in contact with the information would be able to look at the place where they're acting and what law would apply; they wouldn't have to guess whether they were going to affect the US industry.

Rights-holders wary of the law of the place where their licensees do business could engage in self-help in the form of contracts with provisions that choose US law. If the provision were coupled with the requirement that the licensee inform everyone in contact with the secret that it's use will be governed by US law, so much the better.

In addition, there'd be no discrimination amongst rights holders. American firms and foreign firms could both use section 1337 and the DTSA. Their claims would be decided in the same way. Using a choice of law rule that pointed to the place with the closest connection and the greatest interest in the relevant issue.

There are two complications. First, the ALI is busily restating conflict laws and foreign relations laws yet again. I think this is the fourth restatement, and it's rejecting the interest analysis approach it's been using and adopting an effect assess—US law will apply if the effect is on the United States. If that approach is adopted, we're back to square one.

Even if we can use an interest analysis, there's a second issue. While there's now no problem under the TRIPS Agreement, there's a potential problem under the WTO's general agreement on tariffs and trad, the GATT, which also has non-discrimination provisions. The difference is that where TRIPS looks at rights holders, the GATT looks at the origin of products.

If we apply a conflicts rule that looks to the state with the greatest interest, goods from a country that has trade secrecy law is very protective of rights-holders would be treated differently from identical goods that come from a country that's more protective of the public domain.

The question then, is whether a choice of law analysis is GATT compatible. There's a general exception to the GATT that excludes laws necessary to secure compliance with the protection of patents, trademarks and copyrights, and to prevent deceptive practices.

But, does the protection of trade secrets fall within that provision? Trade secrets aren't mentioned. Is a law that uses a conflicts analysis in its implementation necessary as required by section D? To my mind, the exception clause should apply; but WTO panels tend to be very formalistic, so they might not see it my way. I would also argue that it makes no sense to consider a choice of law rule within the antidiscrimination provisions of the GATT.

Countries sacrifice sovereignty when they enter an international agreement. But as long as they adopt substantive law that is consistent with the agreement, they should expect that their choices will prevail within their own territories. That's what the Supreme Court is aiming at with its presumption against extraterritoriality, and it's a result that can be achieved with the conflicts approach that adopts an interest analysis.

Unfortunately, I still have to convince Linda and my trade college and the AOI to adopt a special rule for IP if it moves to the effects test as a general matter. I'm counting on Susy and the rest of this panel and all of you to perhaps help me find a better approach. Thank you.

III. Christoph Rademacher

Professor Christoph Rademacher: Good morning. I would also like to thank the organizers and in particular, Sharon Sandeen for setting up this wonderful conference. We had Sharon at our place, at our university in Tokyo a few years ago, and while we were in the midst of discussing a revision of Japanese trade secret protection—trade secret law—so she was delivering valuable input.

I'm more than pleased to share a little bit of the experience of how trade secret law was changed in Japan in the last years, in the last decades, to provide a bit of a comparative context—a comparative element. Also, maybe to tag along a little bit on what Professor Dreyfuss mentioned on the identical nature of trade secret protection, in your case it was and in TianRui, it was US and China.

Let's talk a little bit about how Japan developed to see whether it's identical or not. I think we can jump from there then to China and the next step.

As many of you may not be aware, 30 years ago—which is a long time ago, but at that time the UTSA wasn't enacted and the US had looked back already on about 200 years of trade secret protection. There was no trade secret protection in Japan. The reasons for this being manifold, I think the main reason was that the Japanese work force was very loyal. Basically, there was no employment mobility, no significant employment mobility in Japan. Companies simply didn't care about protecting their trade secret as they wouldn't have to face the situations that people would leave and take their know-how and their trade secrets with them.

It's not that Japan was a developing country back in these days, also not an IP point of view, compared, for example with the US in the '80s towards the '90s, Japan has significantly more patent applications, so Japanese companies are very much aware of the need to protect its property. Just trade secret protection was nothing that they were too crazy to get into, as they found themselves frequently on the defending end of trade secret losses in the United States, and there was no interest to create another phase of litigation back on their home turfs in Japan.

Things started to change a little bit in the '80s when the lifetime tenure system gradually started to erode; employees started to look into doing other things—pursuing other careers in the midst of their tenure at their company. Asian economies which were not really relevant in the technology area before the 1980s started to emerge, started to compete. Technology transfer into China, into Taiwan, into Formosa and to Korea started to become relevant.

In particular in the beginning, Korean companies were quite savvy about recruiting Japanese engineers to work towards the end of their careers, making them attractive packages—attracting offers—and thereby started to delve into the know-how of the Japanese companies. Japanese industries started to be a little bit more interested in protecting trade secrets.

Also, the topic came up during the discussion of the TRIPS Agreement as to the US was pushing for trade secret protection as part of TRIPS, as also Professor Dreyfuss mentioned earlier. Japan found it increasingly difficult, as it was aligned with the US and with the EU on most other points, to make a plausible or good case against some minimal trade secrets protection. When it became clear that TRIPS would include a chapter, or at least an article, on trade secret protection, Japan started to prepare itself in earnest to roll out trade secret protection also, domestically.

So, in 1990, the Unfair Competition Prevention Act in Japan was revised for the first time, including a definition of trade secret. Trade secret misappropriation was introduced as an act of unfair competition, as a special tort, and trade secrets as such were defined in Article 2, vi, of the Act as being technical or business information useful for commercial activities such as manufacturing or marketing methods that were kept secret and not publicly known. So, those of you who are familiar with the UTSA trade secret definition, I think we can see some similarities.

Also, the Act went on to define those acts of unfair competition involving trade secrets, as basically the wrongful acquisition of trade secrets, as wrongful use of trade secrets that were being wrongfully acquired, or as the disclosure of a trade secret in breach of legal duty to maintain secrecy. Basically, three types of unfair competition: wrongful acquisition, wrongful use, or wrongful disclosure.

Between 1990 and 2015, we had a number of amendments to the UCPA and to other laws governing or being related to trade secrets. A trade secret owner could file a civil action in a court with some technical knowledge, which would be the IP Division at the Tokyo District Court, and that was, at least when it was rolled out, thought to be relevant.

It didn't really attract too much action, so there was a procedure tool to have an in camera proceeding where, of course, the trade secret owner would have to disclose what the trade secret is in the course of the proceedings. They could seek confidential treatment of these documents and also of the court hearing in order to make sure that the trade secret would not be disclosed, at least in theory. A lot of procedural tools in Japan come from Europe, and at least from a European point of view, that would have been quite advanced.

Looking into trade secret litigation, most trade secret owners who brought actions and civil actions were not very successful. We did a study a few years ago where we looked into all trade secret litigation that was filed in the Tokyo and Osaka District Court, and you can see that in most cases, the trade secret owner—or the person named to have a trade secret—would not prevail. The reason most often being that the Court took a relatively strict approach on looking into whether the information was really properly governed, kept secret, in order to constitute a trade secret. In many cases, they found that that was not the case.

The topic of the panel—the extraterritorial reach of trade secrets—Japan started its process of properly thinking about the nature of trade secret protection back in 2013-2014. This thought process was triggered again by two high-profile cases which were international in nature. There was a case of Nippon Steel and Sumitomo, a Japanese steel manufacturer that alleged the misappropriation of material production know-how by a Korean former joint venture partner and competitor.

There was a Toshiba case. Toshiba, one of the early manufacturers and innovators in the area of ram, amongst other things, of memory chip production and design, alleged that Hynix, a Korean competitor, misappropriated significant data and technical know-how related to the production of memory chips.

In both cases, there were engineers of the Japanese companies who were later found that they had disclosed information to the Korean business competitors and that cost a significant outflow of technical know-how to the Japanese companies; it kind of changed the market positions. Of course, it was also marketed in a way that it gave a nice public outcry and maybe started to become active.

In 2014-2015, METI, the Japanese Ministry of Economy, Technology and Industry, prepared a change of the UCPA. Amongst other things, it expanded criminal liabilities. The graph I showed you earlier was only talking about civil cases. While there had been the possibility of criminal sanctions and criminal prosecution in Japan, that was not really much used, as prosecutors and police didn't really want to get involved into something as esoteric as trade secret misappropriation.

Amongst other things, the scope of criminal liability was expanded to international, to extraterritorial conduct. So, even before a wrongful use or wrongful disclosure outside Japan had been subject to Japanese criminal law, but now also the conduct of wrongful acquisition was made subject to Japanese criminal law.

In addition, there were a few other elements that were changed. For example, criminal liability for attempted misappropriation was included, not only completed misappropriation. The fine for trade secret misappropriation was increased, and there was an increase or the possibility to increase the fine in the case of misappropriation that would negatively affect the Japanese economy through international or foreign conduct. In this case, there was the probability to have up to a billion yen against companies, and 30 million yen fine against individuals.

The possibility was introduced that the prosecutor could start prosecution of trade secret misappropriation without having a complaint by the injured party, which was a requirement before.

Another thing that was introduced more recently, was the system of board of measures. The TianRui case was watched with quite some curiosity in Japan as—prior to this 2014 amendment, there was no board of measures available to stop the import of trade secret misappropriating goods, so in 2015, the idea of the board of measures system was rolled out. It was specified a little bit more throughout 2015 and actually this year, 2017, the new board of measures, the new custom procedure was introduced.

Kind of interesting, a little bit different from the board of measures that had been in place for patent and for trademark infringing goods—this was under a two-step procedure. First of all, somebody who suspects that a competitor or somebody they expect would be importing trade secret misappropriating goods, then in the first step, this person would need to obtain an infringement option from the Ministry, from the IP department within METI. Only upon convincing METI that there's really a likelihood of trade secret misappropriation through importation, then could you request seizure of goods through the custom authorities upon arrival of the goods in a Japanese port or airport.

After such seizure, there would be a notification of such seizure and an initial determination by the custom authorities. There could be a consultation with the relevant part of the METI, again; if considered infringing, there would be an import stop. Then, of course, if the importer would insist there was no trade secret misappropriation going on in the creation of those products and the manufacture of those products, then there would be a lawsuit at the Tokyo or the Osaka District Court.

In a way, this is not so different maybe from the export procedure that the DTSA rolled out in the United States, and this is basically a procedural tool that an information owner could resort to stop, in an international cross-border context, the importation of goods into Japan.

I think I want to stop here and pass onto the next person in the panel. This, as a comparative background and an interesting showcase how a trade secret protection can be ramped up in a country within 20 or 30 years, often following examples of the US development. Thank you very much.

IV: Susy Frankel

Professor Susy Frankel: Hello. Thank you. First, I would like to begin with thanking Professor Sandeen, who is now here to my right. Thank you very much, Sharon, for inviting me to this event.

You can think of my job is to, along with my panelists, bring the rest of the world into the room. In fact, everything I know about trade secrets really comes from Sharon Sandeen; she has extreme extraterritorial reach of her work in trade secret law. What I don't know from Sharon, I know from Rochelle's work in international intellectual property, and also from Elizabeth Rowe, who spoke a little earlier—her joint work with Sharon.

I'm actually not really a trade secrets lawyer, so you might say to yourself, "So, what is this New Zealander who is saying she is not a trade secrets lawyer doing here?" My main area of research is international intellectual property rules and the interpretation of the TRIPS Agreement.

I'm going to spend a bit of time referring to the provisions that we've heard about here from both Rochelle's and Christoph's talks, and expand on those a little, and give, if you like, a little bit of the perspectives from some of those extraterritorial places. Of course, they don't consider themselves extraterritorial, right?

I'm going to focus a little bit on some of the trade negotiation dynamics that occur. Of course, as Rochelle mentioned in her talk, there is a number of difficulties internationally with trade secrets; indeed, of course, I come from a breach of confidence jurisdiction.

Some of you will know that is essentially the rest of the common law world—the other parts of the common law, and these doctrines, whilst they have a relationship between each other, and Nari Lee will talk more about the EU in that context. Of course, whether England remains part of the EU is another question and another difficult out there. But these doctrines, while they don't particularly net very well onto each other.

There's nothing quite like the notion of extraterritorial application of US law that makes sense from a US business point of view, that really doesn't make a lot of good international relations. Rochelle mentioned, in particular, a UK case where the idea was, "Hold on a minute; we're not having that ruling for a UK business."

What can we do about this situation, and what can we observe about the different approaches around the world? I'm going to refer back to GATT XX, a provision that Rochelle mentioned in her talk. I'm going to begin there.

This provision really is an exception to the idea of the nondiscrimination principles in GATT, as Rochelle mentioned. Just to remind you—for those of you who don't read the GATT Agreement daily. What is this exception about?

It really says, "Look, okay. Sometimes in making laws and regulations you have to do things that look a little discriminatory, right?" You work for your national businesses. How do you overcome that? Rochelle mentioned that there's this provision—the exception, indeed, and it doesn't specifically refer to trade secrets.

The GATT Agreement was written first in 1947; it was a post-war agreement that was designed to bring about security. Then it was re-enacted in the WTO in 1994. At that time, the TRIPS Agreement became part of the WTO's single undertaking. I would argue that one of the things that can be done with this provision is to read the intellectual property part widely.

This argument I would base not only on the text that it refers in subparagraph there to including those relating to and highlighted patents, trademarks and copyrights, but also because when treaties are interpreted—believe it or not, there is an international agreement that is also part of the WTO about how you interpret treaties, and that is the Vienna Convention on the Law of Treaties. You read that these clauses, not only by their ordinary meaning, but also take into account object and purpose.

That's a huge area that I won't have time to go into at the moment, but I would push against the formalism of the WTO that Rochelle referred to, to take on what is often described as the wholistic part of the WTO, to read this to include trade secrets as an exception. Why do that?

Because it doesn't make a lot of sense, really to say, "Part of the TRIPS Agreement is relevant to this exception, and other parts of it aren't." So, turning to the TRIPS Agreement itself in Article 39 that has a couple of mentions. Referring here, of course, this is the article that Rochelle referred to as having bare bones. I want to focus a little bit on what some of those bare bones are, and why I think they're likely to remain bare on the international stage.

We had this idea that you have effective protection against unfair competition and protecting undisclosed information. Already, there is WTO jurisprudence about the word, "effective." From a plaintiff's point of view, you might think effective protection is protection where you can bring a case and have enforcement. But the WTO, in the Tyner** enforcement case brought by the US against China did not take that view of the equivalent sort of wording in another part of TRIPS that was there. That was Article 41 of TRIPS and the use of effective.

So, effective isn't a plaintiff-centric or in today's WTO's state-centric approach; rather, it's effective to a certain extent within national law. What does unfair competition mean? That is, of course, a very EU-driven concept, and I won't spend my time on that.

What does undisclosed information mean? We also know, under paragraph 2, that this action allows—that the TRIPS Agreement at least requires countries protect the laws to a reasonable degree, providing the information is secret, has commercial value, and so on. Of course, these terms are all somewhat subjective. How do you define them?

They're subjective on a jurisdiction by jurisdiction basis. This provision has a footnote—footnote 10—which really brings us to the core of the international difficulty. The purpose of this provision, "a manner contrary to honest commercial practices" shall mean at least practices such as breach of contract, breach of confidence and inducement to breach, and includes the acquisition of undisclosed information.

Another way of reading this footnote is that it includes all variance on common law breach of confidence, all variance on common law contract, and of course, there's also this important intersection with employment law.

If there's anything that is jurisdictionally specific and that countries do not like to agree to standards internationally, it is the area of employment law, or indeed, labor law, where you can call it different things. Once you combine intellectual property with issues of employment law, and the notion that some countries because they are large economies should have extraterritorial reach of the law, you have what is known as one of those things that it's really hard to negotiate internationally.

One of the interesting developments in the trans-Pacific partnership that was, was that it actually attempted to have both an IP chapter with trade secret definitions, and an employment chapter. I'm going to return to the TPP that was, shortly, and discuss whether it was a good method to overcome some of this difficulty.

Why does this diversity of laws matter? It matters, of course, because if you are an international business, if you are part of a global value network, then you may actually want some consistency around the world. As a general rule, I'm not in favor of detailed harmonization, largely because I think it's important that countries can adjust to their particular economic needs.

One of the problems with this provision and Article 29 of the TRIPS Agreement—sorry. It should really be 39; I think I had a little plane lapse on the number. Excuse that. I suddenly thought, "How did I lose 10 articles?"

Of course, it's relationship with the national treatment principle. National treatment is incredibly important, as Rochelle mentioned, because it's about how foreigners should be able to bring action in national courts. That, of course, works within the US, and the US businesses also want that ability outside of the US. That is one of the points of agreements such as the TRIPS Agreement.

National treatment really works hand in hand with minimum standards. When you have something that is a minimum standard defined as broadly as Article 39 and its footnote, you really actually don't have a minimum standard at all. What you have is a collection of diverse national laws. In that situation, national treatment really largely becomes slightly malfunctioning. But, nonetheless, it continues to apply. It applies to the scope, maintenance and enforcement of laws.

One question that arises is whether trade secret protection and the style of trade secret protection that is found here in the US—of course, I appreciate that state variability in it as well—whether that is actually caught in any way by the TRIPS Agreement. The TRIPS Agreement doesn't actually define intellectual property except by saying, "intellectual property means all the things within the TRIPS Agreement." So, it means Article 39, as well as the other things within there.

Why does this matter? Because if trade secrets are within the TRIPS Agreement, then members of the TRIPS Agreement have to apply trade secret law on this national treatment non-discrimination basis. However, if you say trade secrets without the TRIPS Agreement, so they're not fully caught by the TRIPS Agreement, then you have the idea that you can have discrimination in the sense that you can treat nationals from different countries differently. That is, of course, the antithesis of global cooperation, but we do see this occurring in some countries.

One example is the Database Right, the EU Database Right. It's applied by the EU on a non-national treatment basis, so on a reciprocity basis. Unless you provide that equivalent unfair extraction right, you cannot seek the EU right. The United States in comparison, of course, the Database Right, the United States doesn't have the equivalent—tends to apply a national treatment rule.

The example that I would give of this is in copyright. The copyright term is not uniformly the life of the author plus 70 years, or 70 years around the world, but the United States will, in most situations, will apply that rule. The EU, on the other hand, would say, "Oh, you only have 50 years; you only get 50 years."

This really matters whether you have national treatment or otherwise. When countries can't achieve protection in other countries, this also tends to push them sometimes towards trying to negotiate harmonization worldwide. If trade secrets are without the TRIPS Agreement, national treatment doesn't apply, but because the matter of undisclosed information is referred to within the TRIPS Agreement, I think that, at least to a certain extent, parts of trade secrets are clearly within the scope of the TRIPS Agreement, and national treatment should apply.

Not everyone agrees with that. When you get into areas of enforcement and what level of national treatment is applicable to enforcement, the area gets even more complicated because the obligations in TRIPS with regard to enforcement are not all that detailed. Additionally, of course, when it comes to criminal enforcement, they're even less detailed.

What attempts are happening? This is the beginning of the Trans-Pacific Partnership that was, and you can see on the slide I say, "TPP now active." In fact, although at least from the United States point of view, the Trans-Pacific Partnership is no longer proceeding, although rumors are rife as to whether some of the clauses from the Trans-Pacific Partnership may take place in the new negotiation of NAFTA.

The TPP is not really dead to the rest of the world. It's certainly not going forward in that way, but what has happened is that it's text has been introduced into other trade negotiations. One example—and I stress it's only one, but it's a pretty important one—it's what known as RCEP. Now RCEP is the regional cooperation economic partnership between the Asian countries, or the Southeast Asian countries and six other countries. Those six other countries include Japan, China, Korea, India, Australia and New Zealand.

This is sometimes being referred to as the TPP with China but without the US. It's not quite that simple. Why does this matter? We see this type of attempt to develop the TRIPS provision moving into other trade agreements. In fact, this isn't the way the TRIPS Agreement came about. There wasn't any bilateral and some regional negotiations, and eventually it moved towards this. This is part of a slightly predictable but totally unpredictable international negotiation pattern.

What happened in the TPP? Well, it brings in the TRIPS language; it brings in again the unfair competition language of the Paris Convention, and it reserves to, as a subject matter point—at least in this chapter—trade secrets encompass at a minimum, undisclosed information as provided for in 39 ii of the TRIPS Agreement.

You can see that, within the TPP negotiations between the US and other countries was actually unable to get a definition at least at this end of trade secrets. Continuing with this part of the TPP, subject to paragraph 3, "Each party shall provide for criminal procedures and penalty."

When I'm able to define in further detail what is a trade secret? What is the relationship with labor law, although, as I mentioned, there is a separate labor law chapter in the TPP, but I'm unable to really get harmonization of full extent of law at international level, the TPP did what I think is becoming a common theme—to actually try and develop the side of enforcement.

Whilst that's understandable, it's also very problematic because whilst enforcement, of course, is enormously important, if you still don't have any greater definition about what you're enforcing, then that notion of providing effective protection that the TRIPS Agreement refers to becomes even more difficult. "Oh, you call that a trade secret? We don't call that a trade secret, therefore we don't have to enforce that trade secret." You end up a little bit at square one, but you are creating, if you like, a trajectory to push that international harmonization negotiation.

You can see these are the areas of criminal enforcement that were referred to in the Trans-Pacific Partnership, the unauthorized and willful access to a trade secret I won't read through it all. There is a third paragraph that refers again to limitations on those enforcements. With respect to the X* in paragraph 2, the previous slide, "the party may, as is appropriate"—so that's like, just as you like—a matter of national discretion, "limit the availability of its criminal procedures or limit the level of penalties in one or more of the following cases: where the X are for the purpose of a commercial advantage or financial gain; where the X are related to a product or service in national or international commerce; the X are intended to injure the owner of a trade secret."

So, who is the owner of a trade secret? Where does that take place? You can see that even with these trade agreements, there remains a number of diverse possibilities for enacting this law at jurisdictional level, but you can also see that there is a push to add a bit of flesh to the naked bones of the TRIPS Agreement. That is slow coming.

I'll return to why that is slow coming in wrapping up my comment. It's slow coming because, as I began, the notion of US law governing the world, whilst often it's very true, it's actually the notion that creates quite a lot of push back in trade agreements. With the current lack of clear knowledge outside of the US—I won't comment on in the US—it's not my job as to where trade policy sits in IP at present, then it becomes even more difficult.

I think that we're in this very non-harmonized phase that will continue for a while, but I think we are going to see a greater push towards trying to harmonize something. I'm skeptical about the ability to do that when the roots of these doctrines in other places are so fundamentally different. When we call it IP, it makes a lot of sense to look a little closely—not at detailed harmonization, but at least at something that truly is a minimum standard, like patents in the TRIPS Agreement. There's a lot of jurisdictional variation there, but the bones that are of patent law have more flesh on them than the bones of the undisclosed information provisions.

I think what's linked with labor law is likely to create a considerable push back internationally, but I think that where the push forward will come from is that the US lacks traditionally in its international negotiations having allies with large developed countries, so often whilst the trans-Atlantic debate is quite furious, there is at least a clear move towards greater protection and sometimes drawing in the third axis of Japan.

Trade secrets are actually very interesting and important for businesses deeply embedded in global value networks. In case you're wondering what kind of intellectual property goes on in New Zealand, while a lot of it is connected to the dairy industry, there's also a lot of long-distance manufacturing, high-tech manufacturing that is like the US sent off shore, but a lot of the research occurs in New Zealand. Of course, it's on a much smaller scale. What that's taught me is that when businesses are involved in global value networks, they value trade secret.

One of the things you may know about the TPP is that—or you may not know about the TPP, so I'll have the pleasure of telling you—New Zealand was really at loggerheads with the US over several parts of the TPP. But, the trade secrets part was one of the few where there was a much closer alliance than previously thought. That is because small and medium sized businesses—and of course that means differences around the world—actually are very interested in trade secret protection.

I believe there is a lot of work to be done by the Academy as to actually how trade secrets help businesses—I think Sharon is leading the way with that. Around the world, I think we'll see whether trade secrets really do help innovation, or whether they, in fact, hinder innovation.

If we are going to develop trade secret law internationally, we have to think about what actually is international innovation, and how do trade secrets work in global value networks. Certainly, companies like 3M—and I know that we're hearing from a speaker later—this comes as a company that springs to mind that really the global value network of the trade secret is the great unknown.

This is the area where, if we're going to have international harmonization, we're going to see greater international fracture as around moving trade secrets to do more with labor law and less with IP.

I believe that Sharon believes this is a considerable intellectual property issue, and so my challenge to you is, not only how do we make this work internationally, but is it really intellectual property? I think we need to work on that definition. I'll leave it with a lot of questions. Again, thank you.

V: Nari Lee

Professor Nari Lee: Thank you very much. I'm also going to start this by thanking Sharon. I actually begged her to let me come to this event because I've been studying—unlike the introduction that was given, I actually haven't done trade secret law for a long time; I've been doing international trade law and trade and IP law.

Trade secret is something that I started studying when Sharon visited Finland, two or three years ago when she visited. When she started talking about trade secret, I realized that this is something that I have to start studying. Coincidentally, that was the time when we started to discuss more seriously about EU's Trade Secret Directive. That's the point of my presentation today.

I don't have to tell you details of this Directive because there is a wonderful article written by Sharon. I'm going to add two more points to that, why it is problematic. One is a question that is related to enforcement, and another is a question that is related with the definition. It ties very nicely with the discussion that Susy just started.

Firstly, the Directive. The Directive was adopted 2016, last year, summer. Member states of the European Union have to transpose this international law by next year, summer. I think there's one member state already—Denmark, I think has proposed the bill to its Parliament that changed its law. Many other member states are working on implementing this Directive into their national law.

It contains a whole bunch of articles on substantive aspects on the protection of trade secret within European Union with the aim of harmonizing protection of trade secret within European Union, and this being a Directive—not being a regulation—it is a harmonization. It is meant to be worded generally in a way leaving some room for member states to implement it in the way they fit in their national law.

As I put on this slide, it contains 40 versatiles, the preamble paragraph. It also shows that there are a lot of justifications and political compromises that have been made in terms of justifying, why we need this Directive. I read through all the preambles very closely, and looked at this work that was on the on the way—various proposal. It's still very unclear what was the point of this Directive other than this purpose to harmonize trade secret protection within the European Union.

The two main things, if you read the versatiles carefully, is that trade secret protection is very important for European businesses; therefore, we need harmonization, and so on and so forth. Two things that come very clear is that it aims to harmonize actually the definition of trade secret among the member states of the European Union, trade secret law, and also provide remedies that are available for the misappropriation of trade secrets in a harmonized manner.

In both accounts, in my opinion as a desktop academic, it failed to provide harmonization for both definitions, in terms of enforcement of those remedies that it actually included in this Directive.

In the interest of time, I'm not going to talk so much about the definition part of it. I'm going to look more on the harmonization of the enforcement aspect of this Directive aims to bring. Because of the very fact that the definition is very broad and contains definitions on trade secret misappropriation and lawful appropriation and lawful uses, as well as unlawfulness, why the underlying ground for trade secret misappropriation, it contains a bunch of articles on that. Because of the very fact that the nature of what this protection is, as Susy said, is it an IP? Is it a property right? Is it a contractual right? Is it a breach of confidence?

The very fact that there is no harmonization, that aspect of trade secret protection in this Directive, and member states are basically free to choose which type of right that they would like to give, as long as these particular conducts are prohibited as an unlawful conduct. Because of that freedom, there is no harmonization on the nature of the right, that makes it very difficult to enforce this right in a harmonized manner. There is no uniform harmonized rule on that. Member states can decide.

There are debates ongoing after Directive text has been adopted, whether it is still IP, or it is not an IP, or whether it is something entirely different. Because many of the member states at the time of the adoption of this Trade Secret Protection Directive have embedded this trade secret protection in their unfair competition law, criminal law, employment law or labor law, and the scope of the Directive is such that it covers only civil and commercial matters, it only harmonizes only a tiny part of this protection.

The part concerning the trade secret enforcement contains some kind of minimum level of remedies as a matter of civil redress. Criminal sanctions that are provided by member states' criminal law cannot be harmonized because you do not have a mandate to harmonize criminal law of the EU member states.

Civil remedies, civil redress only are included in this harmonization Directive. It includes a minimum level of remedies that should be available for the member states in the member states as a civil redress for the violation of trade secret protection. There are no rules concerning how these remedies should be enforced.

If I show you versatile 37 of the preamble, the "Directive does not aim to establish harmonized rules for judicial cooperation, jurisdiction, the recognition and enforcement judgments in civil and commercial matters, or deal with applicable law. Other union instruments which govern such matters in general terms, should in principle, remain equally applicable to the field covered by this Directive."

There is no rule that deals with the enforcement of—to get to this remedy, so the enforcement of the trade secret protection. This creates a problem because there is actually a uniform rule in European Union concerning choice of forum, concerning civil and commercial matters, called VERSA Regulation, and room one** and room two** regulations: regulations meaning that the law of the European Union, not Directive harmonizing, but uniform law that decides on applicable law.

Whether trade secret falls under these two regulations, or under three, actually—there are layers of regulations—or whether it should be classified as IP, which actually contains a different set of rules in exceptions in this regulation, but has to be decided first. That creates a complexity in terms of enforcement.

As Rochelle showed with her presentation beautifully, there are a lot of extraterritorial enforcements that have to be done in trade secret protection, and none of that is reflected in this Directive. Not only does it fail to deliver a uniform definition of the right—what is the nature of the right? It doesn't say what that right is; it doesn't say anywhere that trade secret should be protected as intellectual property.

It actually says in versatile 6 that it is, to the contrary, that no new exclusive right should be created based on this. Member states are not obliged to create new exclusive rights. Member states may choose to do so, if they want to, but they are not obliged to create a new exclusive right. There is no definition on the nature of the right. No new means of enforcing this new set of remedies that are actually provided under this Directive.

That is problematic in a way because of the fact that some of this, as Sharon has beautifully shown in her article, in Article 4 this initial definition of unlawfulness. There are several places where new types of unlawfulness seem to be introduced. One of them is Article 4, paragraph 5, "importation of goods that may be embodying trade secret information."

That importation rule creates a problem because of the fact that that requires border measures to be somehow regulated, and that goods importing into a European Union member state has to be some how regulated. That seems to be a new type of law, and how that has to be enforced, is not clearly defined.

It is also an interesting angle that this Directive brings about, because it's ambivalent about whether it's IP or not IP, existing rules on the forum choices that was applied to cross-border injunction—that's basically what probably litigants want within European Union. That rule may change after this Directive is adopted.

What do I mean by this? Under the Brussels Regulations, Article 8, when there are multiple defendants, then this close connection rule allowed in a way that multiple right holders or claim holders can initiate the litigation in one court, combining all the litigation and allowing the court that sees the jurisdictions to be able to issue or hear a case with multiple defendants.

That clause was used in patent infringement litigation for some time. You may have heard about this by Dutch court, particularly, issuing cross-border injunctions, 10 European injunctions, provisional injunctions, cross-border injunctions using this clause. The European Court of Justice put a stop to that in 2003. The Roche v. Primus case, and two other patent cases where this close connection rule in terms of foreign selections were not allowed.

This was the patent case, and now because of the very fact that this is not patent, will this Directive not allow when there is a claim for trade secret, will it be now be used using Article 8 of the Brussels Regulations that deals with the questions that are related with the civil and commercial matters? Litigations. That is one of the interesting angles that this Directive brings about.

There are also many questions that are related to the applicable law, as well as the forum selections that are regulated under Brussels Regulation. In the interest of time, I'm not going to go into detail. What I want to highlight with this presentation is that there is a push to harmonize within the European Union with the assumptions that there have been 20 years of exercise with TRIPS Agreement with the skeletal definition of trade secret, and therefore it was possible to harmonize this trade secret.

With this Directive, the text and the whole process of how this text was adopted and the problems that it would present the member states to implement, this Directive shows that harmonization of trade secret is a very difficult project. It would lead to a situation as the text adopted by this Directive shows, that you cannot help wondering whether harmonization of trade secret protection is altogether possible at all.

In the end, this is not something that is like an intellectual property right that is clearly neutrally definable according to some objective rules. It is something that falls between property rules as well as contracts, based like a private order in practices, as well.

It raises a lot of questions, and it doesn't in the end, harmonize either the definition or the means of enforcing the trade secret protection for the EU member states. That's all I have to say. Thank you very much.

VI. Discussion

Professor Sandeen: Alissa reminded me I'm listed as the moderator, so I'm going to moderate. We might have time for questions. We're on time; we started a little late.

Hearing everybody's presentations, first of all, I love puzzles. Now you know why I love international intellectual property law, or international trade law. It's this huge puzzle, and if I were to summarize the theme of what I heard from everybody is that it's really easy to say in the abstract, "Gee, we need to harmonize trade secret law internationally. Let's just, in the case of the EU—TRIPS before it, but then the EU Trade Secret Directive, we've basically said, "Let's take US law mainly based on the Uniform Trade Secrets Act and let's require all countries to adopt it."

The problem is that you're not writing on a blank slate. Even if they adopt that law, there are always these other things that come into play, including other laws, other treaties, social norms, and so forth. I agree with the conclusion that the ability to actually harmonize trade secret law from a point of view where companies can be sure that, if they have a trade secret in the United States, it will be recognized in Japan or Finland, or whatever, is really problematic. That's not because those countries don't want to protect trade secrets, it's just because they have other issues going on.

With that, let me see if there are any questions from the audience that I can ask, repeat. This is that pause, like in class when I ask a question.

Okay. Let me repeat that. Where does the EU stand with respect to trade secret law? I'll let Nari talk about that.

Professor Lee: There is a new Directive that was adopted 2016 that has to be implemented in national law by next year, summer. All the member states of the EU are changing their trade secret law at this point—drafting, re-drafting their law statutes—reviewing them at least, to figure out how to implement this 15 Articles or more—procedural matters also into their national law.

To answer your question in a more practical manner, does it change a lot? No, it actually doesn't change a lot.

Professor Sandeen: If I may, Nari, for those of you who aren't aware of EU law, the basic point is a directive directs countries to adopt laws that comply with the directive. Each country's laws can be slightly different. Built into the directive usually is what they call international flexibilities where you have choices that you can make.

What's going on in Europe is that they currently have some principles—Nari and Susy alluded to it—under different areas of law: unfair competition, labor law, a sui generis law in Sweden, for instance, and they have to make a decision of whether their existing laws comply with the Directive or not. If they decide, no, then they might adopt supplemental law.

Christoph and I were at a program in Munich in November where the other speaker opined that Germany is probably is not going to change its law; it will simply conclude that its law complies with the Directive.

I don't know if you want to add anything.

Professor Lee: That's something as I was trying to point out because of the fact that this Directive does not add so much useful. There are, of course, very important declaratory statements that are made that it's related with the freedom of information and rights of generalist and whether trade secrets should cover or not, so that as a minimum rule.

Because of the fact that it doesn't really necessarily change anything dramatically, some member state might choose not to change their laws almost at all. Some member states may have to change the law and at least introduce the definition. Maybe they might consider that their case law—some member states don't even have a definition of trade secret, but based on their case law—court decisions only, they might have to provide a statute. That's something that member states have freedom to decide because it is a directive.

Professor Sandeen: Susy, in one minute tell Wayne why there are problems in trade negotiations.

Professor Frankel: As Travis indicated, it's a huge question. If I focus particularly on the trade secrets, it occurred to me with the previous question, we tend to think of patent law as very diverse around the world, but if you plot things on a totally diverse law to harmonized continuum. The purpose of international negotiations actually is often to point towards harmonization, but not to reach itz The flexibilities allow you to adjust and calibrate to domestic needs, which may be to import innovation, or it may be to locally grow that innovation. It may be to enter into global value networks, right?

I think the most contentious area of IP for the TRIPS Agreement has been around patent and particularly around pharmaceuticals. Even though there is a lot of diversity and a lot of debate around that, it's considerably more harmonized than trade secrets. It's considerably further toward this harmonization, so whilst you're still going to get very diverse results even within this country, and so on.

There are certain pin pointers of common norms. It doesn't exist in trade secrets. One of the great suspicions internationally, and whether it's true or not, is partly beside the point, is that when a country such as this one moves from pushing patent law into also pushing trade secret law, then other countries are like, "Well, actually, we like patents because that's all open and that's global disclosure." You have a disjuncture between the reality for business and the trade rhetoric.

The important nexus between those—and then I will stick to the one minute—is that the reality is that something doesn't look like a trade secret in one place, necessarily—and it doesn't mean that that place has pirates. It doesn't mean that they're taking the technology and misusing it or misappropriating it; rather, what is secret about it? Wouldn't it be good if we could use it to follow an innovation to make a better product for local circumstances? To make products more available. That, I would say, is the biggest tension: how does everyone get their piece of the innovation game?

Professor Sandeen: I'll let Rochelle conclude.

Professor Dreyfuss: I'll put it more bluntly: some countries are information importers and some countries are information exporters. The countries that are information exporters want strong protection for the information they create; the countries that are net information importers see this as a tax on public welfare and their ability to access information. As Susy says, build on it for their own particular needs. It's very hard to get agreement amongst those different countries.

Professor Sandeen: I'll make one concluding remark related to that. That's why Benjamin Franklin was a copyright infringer.

We want one more question?

Professor Dreyfuss: There's a case about Kevlar taking of DuPont's Kevlar secret—Kolon against DuPont, in which we applied US law and tell this Korean company they couldn't make Kevlar, even in Korea. There are different ways that you can parse this; you could say US law applies as far as the US market is concerned, but a US can't tell the Kolon company what they can and can't do in Korea. They can't supply Kevlar to the Korean army? That's a big step.

I think there are some cases, but they're not completely harmonized. They show a lot of different approaches, and we have to think about what the right approach is under the DTSA where there probably is a little bit more scope to apply US law extraterritorially. Whether that's a good thing to do or not.

How South Korea's Improper Solicitation and Graft Act (Kim Young-ran Act) Can Help Protect US Trade Secrets

By Lana Rask.[1]

I. Introduction 209
II. United States Corruption Ranking versus South Korean
    Corruption Ranking 210
   A. Corruption 210
       1. Corruption Perceptions Index 210
       2. Control of Corruption 211
       3. Global Corruption Barometer 211
       4. OECD Anti-Bribery Convention 212
III. Trade Secrets 213
   A. Definition 213
   B. Importance of trade secrets 214
IV. Trade Secrets in the United States 214
   A. How the US defines trade secrets 214
       1.   The Uniform Trade Secrets Act (UTSA) 214
V. Trade Secrets in South Korea 215
   A. How South Korea defines trade secrets 215
       1. Unfair Competition Prevention and Trade Secrets
          Protection Act (UCPA) 215
       2. Act on Prevention of Divulgence and
          Protection of Industrial Technology (Industrial Technology Act) 216
       3. Impact on United States Businesses 217
   B. Controlling law between the United States and Korea 217
       1. United States-Korea Free Trade Agreement (KORUS) 217
       2. Trade-Related Aspects of Intellectual Property (TRIPS) 218
VI. Corporate Espionage 219
   A. Corporate Espionage 219
       1. Corporate espionage cases involving trade secrets between the United
          States and South Korea 221
VII. Improper Solicitation and Graft Act 222
   A. Background to the Improper Solicitation and Graft Act 222
       1. Bribery 223
       2. Kim Young-ran Act 226
       3. Concerns about the Kim Young-ran Act 227
       4. Reactions to the Kim Young-ran Act 229
       5. Future of US businesses working with South Korea 229
VIII. Conclusion 230

---

[1] Lana Rask is a Mitchell Hamline Juris Doctor student expected to graduate in 2018.

I. INTRODUCTION

Trade secrets are the lifeblood of many companies. Some of the best kept trade secrets in the United States are the recipe for Coca-Cola, Colonel Sanders' spice blend for KFC chicken, and the formula for WD-40.[2] A law article published in the *New York Law Journal* states that "Theft of trade secrets is likely the most pressing threat to the security of sensitive information maintained by U.S. companies."[3] In fact, according to the Commission on the Theft of American Intellectual Property, "[t]he annual losses are likely to be comparable to the current annual level of U.S exports to Asia—over $300 billion."[4] Congress has passed and amended laws aimed at protecting businesses' trade secrets. One of the most recent examples is an added amendment to the Economic Espionage Act.[5]

"On December 28, 2012, President Obama signed into law the Theft of Trade Secrets Clarification Act, which amends and expands the Economic Espionage Act (EEA)."[6] This amendment, which received overwhelming support from both the Senate and the House of Representatives, "amends the EEA so that it now covers trade secret 'related to a product or service used in or intended for use in' commerce."[7] The United States is not the only country that has made increased efforts to protect trade secrets.[8] One of the ways that individuals or businesses try to gain trade secrets is through bribery. Kolon Industries, a South Korean company, used just such tactics to attempt to steal trade secrets from DuPont Inc., an American corporation.[9] In response to growing criticism and concern over the use of bribery, South Korea on September 28, 2016, passed the Improper Solicitation and Graft Act, also known as the Kim Young-Ran Act, to combat bribery.[10]

---

[2] R. Mark Halligan & David A. Haas, *The Secret of Trade Secret Success*, Forbes (Feb. 19, 2010), http://www.forbes.com/2010/02/19/protecting-trade-secrets-leadership-managing-halligan-haas.html.
[3] Daniel A. Schnapp, *Trade Secret Theft and the Rise of the Private Right of Action*, New York Law Journal (Apr. 6, 2015), http://www.foxrothschild.com/publications/trade-secret-theft-and-the-rise-of-the-private-right-of-action/.
[4] THE COMMISSION ON THE THEFT OF AMERICAN INTELLECTUAL PROPERTY: THE IP COMMISSION REPORT (2012), http://www.ipcommission.org/report/IP_Commission_Report_052213.pdf.
[5] Theft of Trade Secrets Clarification Act of 2012, Pub. L. No. 112-236, 126 Stat. 1627.
[6] David E. Dubberly, *New Federal Law Increases Trade Secret Protection*, Nexsen Pruet (Jan. 22, 2013), https://www.nexsenpruet.com/insights/new-federal-law-increases-trade-secret-protection.
[7] *Id.* "The Economic Espionage Act (EEA) was enacted in 1996." In *United States v. Aleynikov*, 737 F. Supp. 2d 173 "the Second Circuit found that Aleynikov had not violated the Economic Espionage Act. The Second Circuit 'interpreted the EEA narrowly to apply only where a trade secret relates to products a company sells, not where it relates to products a company uses internally.' After this case was decided, "Congress passed the Theft of Trade Secrets Clarification Act. . . . by unanimous consent in the Senate and be a vote of 388-4 in the House."
[8] *See, e.g.*, David Vance Lucas, *International Harmonization of Trade Secret Rights and Remedies*, Bradley (Dec. 13, 2016), https://www.bradley.com/insights/publications/2016/12/international-harmonization-of-trade-secret-rights-and-remedies (EU 943, passed on June 8, 2016, "creates the first private common trade secret action applicable in all EU member states").
[9] United States v. Aleynikov, 737 F. Supp. 2d 173 (S.D.N.Y. 2010).
[10] *Legal Update: A Brief Overview of the Anti-Corruption and Bribery Prohibition Act*, Jipyong, (Apr. 6, 2015), http://www.jipyong.com/newsletter_alert/150406/Legal_update.pdf.

This article will explore how the United States compares to South Korea in terms of corruption, including bribery. Next will be a discussion of how the United States defines trade secrets versus how South Korea defines trades secrets. After the discussion of trade secrets, the controlling laws between South Korea and the United States will be examined. Then, this paper shall explore corporate espionage. This section will include an examination of *DuPont Inc. v. Kolon USA Inc.* Finally, this paper will explore the Improper Solicitation and Graft Act of Korea, also known as the Kim Young-Ran Law, recently passed by South Korea and how this law may affect United States' business relations with South Korea.

II. UNITED STATES CORRUPTION RANKING VERSUS SOUTH KOREAN CORRUPTION RANKING

A. Corruption

Transparency International defines corruption as "'the abuse of entrusted power for private gain.' Corruption can be classified as grand, petty and political, depending on the amounts of money lost and the sector where it occurs."[11] Corruption can be found across the globe. "Transparency International states "Sixty-eight percent of countries worldwide have a serious problem. Half of the G20 are among them."[12] Transparency International uses various corruption measurement tools to determine how countries fall on different facets of corruption: the Corruption Perceptions Index, a country's control of corruption, the Global Corruption Barometer, the enforcement of OECD Anti-Bribery Convention, and the Bribe Payers Index.[13]

1. Corruption Perceptions Index

Transparency International uses a Corruption Perceptions Index to measure the corruption found in surveyed countries.[14] Of the 168 countries that Transparency International has gathered data on and ranked, the United States ranks sixteenth along with Austria.[15] The United States received a score of 76/100 on Transparency International's Corruption Perceptions Index.[16] South Korea on the other hand ranks thirty-seventh.[17] South Korea received a score of 56/100 on the Corruption Perceptions Index.[18]

---

[11] WHAT IS CORRUPTION, http://www.transparency.org/what-is-corruption/#define (last visited Nov. 8, 2016). "Transparency International was created in 1993. Their vision is 'a world in which government, business, civil society and the daily lives of people are free of corruption.' Transparency International has 'more than 100 national chapters worldwide and an international secretariat in Berlin.'"
[12] CORRUPTION PERCEPTIONS INDEX 2015, https://www.transparency.org/cpi2015/ (last visited Nov. 8, 2016).
[13] CORRUPTION BY TERRITORY/COUNTRY, https://www.transparency.org/country/KOR (last visited Nov. 9, 2016).
[14] *Id.* "The Corruption Perceptions Index ranks countries/territories based on how corrupt a country's public sector is perceived to be. It is a composite index drawing on corruption-related data from expert and business surveys carried out by a variety of independent and reputable institutions. Scores range from 0 (highly corrupt) to 100 (very clean)."
[15] CORRUPTION BY TERRITORY/COUNTRY, https://www.transparency.org/country/USA (last visited Nov. 9, 2016).
[16] *Id.*
[17] https://www.transparency.org/country/KOR (last visited Nov. 8, 2016).
[18] *Id.*

2. *Control of Corruption*

Transparency International also looks at how well a country is perceived to control corruption.[19] From a survey taken in 2010, the United States is in the 86th percentile with a score of 1.232890271 whereas South Korea is in the 69th percentile with a score of 0.422983221.[20]

3. *Global Corruption Barometer*

Transparency International uses a global corruption barometer (GCB) to show how corruption is viewed on a national level for each country.[21] The 2013 GCB report shows that 53% of respondents in the United States felt that businesses were corrupt or extremely corrupt.[22] Furthermore, 36% of respondents felt that since 2011, the level of corruption in the United States had increased a lot.[23] In South Korea on the other hand, only 33% of respondents felt that businesses were corrupt or extremely corrupt.[24] Only 13% of South Korean respondents felt that the level of corruption in South Korea has increased a lot since 2011.[25]

---

[19] http://www.transparency.org/cpi2010/results (last visited Nov. 9, 2016).
"Control of corruption reflects perceptions of the extent to which public power is exercised for private gain. This includes both petty and grand forms of corruption, as well as 'capture' of the state by elites and private interests. Control of corruption is one of the six dimensions of the Worldwide Governance Indicators. For the given scores, point estimates range from about -2.5 to 2.5. Higher values correspond to better governance outcomes."
[20] *Id.* (last visited Nov. 9, 2016).
[21] https://www.transparency.org/country/USA (last visited Nov. 9, 2016).
"The Global Corruption Barometer is the only worldwide public opinion survey on views and experiences of corruption. It captures how corruption is views at the national level. It also provides a measure of people's experience of corruption for a specified year."
[22] *Global Corruption Barometer: United States*, TRANSPARENCY INTERNATIONAL, https://www.transparency.org/gcb2013/country/?country=united_states (last visited Apr. 6, 2017).
[23] *Id.*
[24] *Global Corruption Barometer: South Korea*, TRANSPARENCY INTERNATIONAL, https://www.transparency.org/gcb2013/country/?country=korea_(south) (last visited Apr. 6, 2017).
[25] *Id.*

4. *OECD Anti-Bribery Convention*

Both the United States and South Korea are signatories to the Organizations for Economic Co-operation and Development (OECD) Anti-Bribery Convention.[26] Transparency International uses data from OECD to rank countries on their enforcement of the OCED Anti-Bribery Convention held in 2011.[27] South Korea falls into the moderate category in terms of enforcement[28] whereas the United States falls into the active category for enforcement.[29]

---

[26] *Our Mission*, THE ORGANISATION FOR ECONOMIC CO-OPERATION AND DEVELOPMENT (OECD), http://www.oecd.org/about/ (last visited Apr. 6, 2017). The OECD was established in 1961 and currently 35 countries are members. According to OECD's website, their mission "is to promote policies that will improve the economic and social well-being of people around the world. The OECD provides a forum in which governments can work together to share experiences and seek solutions to common problems. [They] work with governments to understand what drives economic, social and environmental change. [They also] measure productivity and global flows of trade and investment. [They] analyze and compare data to predict future trends. [They] set international standards on a wide range of things, from agriculture and tax to the safety of chemicals."
[27] https://www.transparency.org/country/KOR (last visited Nov. 9, 2016).
"The country review is based on the progress of the Organization for Economic Co-operation and Development (OECD) Convention on Combating Bribery of Foreign Public Officials in International Business Transactions, requiring each party to make foreign bribery a crime. Countries are evaluated and classified into four categories: active enforcement, moderate enforcement, little enforcement, or no enforcement."
[28] *Id.*
[29] https://www.transparency.org/country/USA (last visited Nov. 9, 2016).

5. Defining Bribery

Looking around the globe, acts of bribery can be found in all if not most countries.[30] Bribery in its simplest form can be defined as "the act or practice of giving or taking a bribe."[31] A bribe is defined as "money or favor given or promised in order to influence the judgment or conduct of a person in a position of trust."[32] Transparency International offers a more in depth definition of bribery.

It defines bribery as, "the offering, promising, giving, accepting or soliciting of an advantage as an inducement for an action which is illegal, unethical or a breach of trust."[33] Transparency International uses the Bribe Payers Index (2011) to measure a country's firms' likelihood to bribe abroad.[34] The United States ranks 10/28 with a score of 8.1[35] on the Bribe Payers Index whereas South Korea ranks 13/28 with a score of 7.9/10 on the Bribe Payers Index.[36]

III. Trade Secret

A. Definition

The general definition given for trade secret from Merriam Webster is: "something (as a formula) which has economic value to a business because it is not generally known or easily discoverable by observation and for which efforts have been made to maintain secrecy."[37] While you can garner the general idea of a what a trade secret is from a dictionary definition, one must look to a countries' individual trade secret law to see how a trade secret is not only defined but what use a trade secret has for companies.

---

[30] *See generally* TRANSPARENCY INTERNATIONAL, http://www.transparency.org/ (last visited Apr. 6, 2017).
[31] *Bribery*, MERRIAM-WEBSTER ONLINE DICTIONARY, http://www.merriam-webster.com/dictionary/bribery (last visited Apr. 6, 2017).
[32] *Bribe*, MERRIAM-WEBSTER ONLINE DICTIONARY, http://www.merriam-webster.com/dictionary/bribe (last visited Apr. 6, 2017).
[33] *Anti-Corruption Glossary*, TRANSPARENCY INTERNATIONAL, https://www.transparency.org/glossary/term/bribery (last visited Apr. 6, 2017).
[34] *Bribe Payers Index*, Transparency International, http://www.transparency.org/bpi2011/results (last visited Apr. 16, 2017). "The Bribe Payers Index ranks the world's wealthiest and most economically influential countries according to the likelihood of their firms to bribe abroad. Scores range from 0 to 10, indicating the likelihood of firms headquartered in these countries to bribe when operating abroad. The higher the score for the country, the lower the likelihood of companies from this country to engage in bribery when doing business abroad."
[35] *Id.*
[36] *Id.*
[37] *Trade Secret*, MERRIAM-WEBSTER ONLINE DICTIONARY, https://www.merriamwebster.com/dictionary/trade%20secret (last visited Dec. 27, 2016).

B. Importance of trade secrets

Trade secrets are the lifeblood of many companies. They can be found in companies that produce food and beverages to companies that produce a substance to dull the surface of new baseballs to even a company that puts out a best-seller list.[38] Without the protection of trade secrets, many companies would not have an advantage over other competitors with similar products. A trade secret can be all that holds a company's existence together.

IV. TRADE SECRETS IN THE UNITED STATES

"Trade Secret law in the United States emerged in the middle of the 19th Century."[39] "The development of trade secret principles arose from cases that were brought to resolve disputes between competitors."[40] Today, we look to the Uniform Trade Secrets Act (UTSA) to define trade secrets in the United States.

A. How the US defines trade secrets

1. The Uniform Trade Secrets Act (UTSA)

The Uniform Trade Secrets Act (UTSA) defines a trade secret as:

> information, including a formula, pattern, compilation, program, device, method, technique, or process, that derives independent economic value, actual or potential, from not being generally known to or readily ascertainable through appropriate means by other persons who might obtain economic value from its disclosure or use; and is the subject of efforts that are reasonable under the circumstances to maintain its secrecy.[41]

As of May 2013, Massachusetts, North Carolina, and New York are the only states that still have not adopted the Uniform Trade Agreement Act.[42] Massachusetts, North Carolina, and New York have individual state statutes for the protection of trade secrets.

---

[38] Melanie Radzicki McManus, "10 Trade Secrets We Wish We Knew, HOW STUFF WORKS: MONEY (Nov. 15, 2011), http://money.howstuffworks.com/10-trade-secrets3.htm.
[39] SHARON K. SANDEEN AND ELIZABETH ROWE, TRADE SECRET LAW IN A NUTSHELL 1 (2013).
[40] Id.
[41] Trade Secret, CORNELL UNIVERSITY LAW SCHOOL: LEGAL INFORMATION INSTITUTE, https://www.law.cornell.edu/wex/trade_secret (last visited Jan. 6, 2017).
[42] Trade Secrets Act, UNIFORM LAW COMMISSION: ACTS, http://www.uniformlaws.org/Act.aspx?title=Trade+Secrets+Act (last visited Jan. 6, 2017).

V. Trade Secrets in South Korea

South Korea first instituted protection of trade secrets in 1961.[43] The Unfair Competition Prevention and Trade Secret Protection Act (UCPA), passed on December 30, 1961,[44] has since been expanded through amendments as trade secrets have become more defined and South Korea has not only participated in trade across the globe but also as Korean businesses have grown.

A. How South Korea defines trade secrets

1. Unfair Competition Prevention and Trade Secrets Protection Act (UCPA)

Article 2.2 of UCPA states "The term 'trade secret' means information, including a production method, sale method, useful technical or business information for business activities, that is not known publicly, is the subject of reasonable efforts to maintain its secrecy, and has independent economic value."[45] The act further goes on to define the term infringement of trade secrets.

> Infringement of trade secrets can mean any of the following acts: (a) An act of acquiring trade secrets by theft, deception, coercion, or other improper means (hereinafter referred to as "act of improper acquisition"), or subsequently using or disclosing the trade secrets improperly acquired (including informing any specific person of the trade secret while under a duty to maintain secrecy; hereinafter the same shall apply);
>
> (b) An act of acquiring trade secrets or using or disclosing the trade secrets improperly acquired, with knowledge of the fact that an act of improper acquisition of the trade secrets has occurred or without such knowledge due to gross negligence;

---

[43] *Unfair Competition Prevention and Trade Secret Protection Act*, WORLD INTELLECTUAL PROPERTY ORGANIZATION: REPUBLIC OF KOREA, http://www.wipo.int/wipolex/en/text.jsp?file_id=188269#LinkTarget_471 (last visited Jan. 6, 2017). According to The World Intellectual Property website, "The World Intellectual Property Organization (WIPO) is a global forum for intellectual services, policy, information and cooperation."
[44] *Id.*
[45] Unfair Competition Prevention and Trade Secret Protection Act, Act No. 5621, Dec. 31, 1998, *amended by* Act No. 14033, Feb. 29, 2016, art. 2 (S. Kor.), *translated in* Korea Legislation Research Institute online database http://elaw.klri.re.kr/eng_mobile/viewer.do?hseq=39690&type=lawname&key=unfair%20competition (last visited Jan. 6, 2017).

(c) An act of using or disclosing trade secrets after acquiring them, with knowledge of the fact that an act of improper acquisition of the trade secrets has occurred or without such knowledge due to gross negligence;

(d) An act of using or disclosing trade secrets to obtain improper benefits or to damage the owner of the trade secrets while under a contractual or other duty to maintain secrecy of the trade secrets;

(e) An act of acquiring trade secrets, or using or disclosing them with the knowledge of the fact that they have been disclosed in the manner provided in item (d) or that such disclosure has been involved, or without such knowledge due to gross negligence;

(f) An act of using or disclosing trade secrets after acquiring them, with the knowledge of the fact that they have been disclosed in a manner provided in item (d) or that such disclosure has been involved, or without such knowledge due to gross negligence.[46]

2. *Act on Prevention of Divulgence and Protection of Industrial Technology (Industrial Technology Act)*

"The Industrial Technology Act was created to address the perceived lack of protection of national core technologies, since the UPCA only protects the trade secrets of private companies."[47] Article 14 of the Industrial Technology Act prohibits:

(1) Acquiring the industrial technology of any institution possessing industrial technology obtained by means of theft, deception, threat, or other unjust means or using or publicizing such industrial technology (including providing information to a specific person in secret; hereinafter the same shall apply);[. . .] (6) Acquiring, merging, etc. industrial technology overseas and failing to report under Article 11-2 (1) and (2) or falsely reporting for the purpose of using national core technology or using it overseas.[48]

---

[46] *Id.*
[47] Peter K. Paik and Kyu-Bin Lim, *Trade Secret Protection in South Korea,* WORLD INTELLECTUAL PROPERTY REVIEW DIGEST (2010). HTTP://WWW.KIMCHANG.COM/USERFILES/FILES/TRADESECRETPROTECTIONINSOUTHKOREA-WORLDIPREVIEW.PDF.
[48] Sogwanbucheo, [Act on Prevention of Divulgence and Protection of Industrial Technology], Act No. 14108, Mar. 29, 2016, http://elaw.klri.re.kr/kor_service/lawView.do?hseq=38483&lang=ENG.

3. *Impact on United States Businesses*

With amendments to both the UCPA and the Industrial Technology Act, the South Korean government is attempting to enforce trade secret laws. With the increase in vigilance by the South Korean government, foreign technology companies doing business in Korea should enhance their internal risk assessment programs.[49] Companies should make plans to guard against any legal consequences that could possibly come—if accused of trade secret theft claims or be involved in an investigation by the Korean government.[50]

B. *Controlling law between the United States and South Korea*

1. *United States—Korea Free Trade Agreement (KORUS)*

The United States—Korea Free Trade Agreement (KORUS)—was enacted on March 15, 2012.[51] This trade agreement with South Korea was "an integral part of President Obama's efforts to increase opportunities for U.S. businesses, farmers and workers through improved access for their products and services in foreign markets."[52] KORUS reaffirms both countries will uphold the existing rights and obligations they have under the TRIPS Agreement.[53]

KORUS also called for both the United States and South Korea to ratify or accede to other Agreements.[54] This Agreement also gives both countries room to use existing laws in place for protection of intellectual property, but also allows for growth and new laws to be used not included in this Agreement. Section 5 states, "A Party may provide more extensive protection for, and enforcement of, intellectual property rights under its law than this Chapter requires, provided that the more extensive protection does not contravene this Chapter."[55] Section five (5) is important, because KORUS does not specifically mention or define trade secrets.

---

[49] *Supra* n. 45, p. 116.
[50] *Id.*
[51] The U.S. —Korea Free Trade Agreement (KORUS), EXPORT.GOV: FREE TRADE AGREEMENTS KOREA, http://2016.export.gov/FTA/korea/index.asp (last visited Jan. 7, 2016) ("On the day of implementation, almost 80 percent of U.S. industrial goods exports to Korea are duty-free including aerospace equipment, agricultural equipment, auto parts, building products, chemicals, consumer goods, electrical equipment, environment goods, travel goods, paper products, scientific equipment and shipping and transportation equipment.").
[52] Why a U.S.-Korea Trade Agreement?, INTERNATIONAL TRADE ADMINISTRATION, http://trade.gov/fta/korea/ (last visited Jan. 7, 2016).
[53] FREE TRADE AGREEMENT BETWEEN THE UNITED STATES OF AMERICA AND THE REPUBLIC OF KOREA,S.Kor.-U.S., March 15, 2012, Chapter Eighteen: Intellectual Property Rights, OFFICE OF THE UNITED STATES TRADE REPRESENTATIVE: TRADE AGREEMENTS https://ustr.gov/sites/default/files/uploads/agreements/fta/korus/asset_upload_file273_12717.pdf. NOTE: Chapter 18, 18.1(2).
[54] *Id.* Paris Convention for the Protection of Industrial Property (1967), the World Intellectual Property Organization (WIPO) Copyright Treaty (1996), and the Trademark Law Treaty (1994).
[55] *Id.*

2. *Trade-Related Aspects of Intellectual Property (TRIPS) Agreement*

The Uniform Trade Secret Act, along with each state's regulations on trade secrets, is not the only protection that United States businesses have. The United States as a member of the World Trade Organization (WTO) is also subject to the Trade-Related Aspects of Intellectual Property Rights Agreement (TRIPS). South Korea, as a member of the WTO is also subject to the TRIPS Agreement. "The TRIPS Agreement, which came into effect on January 1, 1995, is to date the most comprehensive multilateral agreement on intellectual property."[56] Copyright and related rights, trademarks, geographical indications, industrial designs, patents, layout-designs of integrated circuits, and undisclosed information are the areas of intellectual property that TRIPS covers.[57]

Trade secrets by definition are undisclosed information. Undisclosed information is required to benefit from protection under the TRIPS Agreement.[58] Article 39.2 states "the protection must apply to information that is secret, that has commercial value because it is secret and that has been subject to reasonable steps to keep it secret."[59] This agreement allows for civil and administrative procedures and remedies.[60] Both injunctions and damages are available as options to parties seeking relief.[61]

---

[56] Overview: the TRIPS Agreement, WORLD TRADE ORGANIZATION: TRIPS: A MORE DETAILED OVERVIEW OF THE TRIPS AGREEMENT, https://www.wto.org/english/tratop_e/trips_e/intel2_e.htm (last visited Jan. 6, 2017) ("The World Trade Organization (WTO) deals with global rules of trade between nations. Its main function is to ensure that trade flows as smoothly, predictably and freely as possible.").
[57] *Id.*
[58] *Id.*
[59] *Id.*
[60] Enforcement of Intellectual Property Rights, WORLD TRADE ORGANIZATION: OVERVIEW: THE TRIPS AGREEMENT, https://www.wto.org/english/tratop_e/trips_e/intel2b_e.htm#civiland (last visited Jan. 6, 2017). Note: Could for use for information of what kind of remedies and procedures are available. Pretty extensive section under the heading on the website.
[61] *Id.*

VI. CORPORATE ESPIONAGE

A. *Corporate Espionage*

Corporate espionage, also known as industrial espionage, can be defined as: "attempting to obtain trade secrets by dishonest means, as by telephone or computer-tapping, infiltration of a competitor's workforce, etc."[62] Corporate espionage occurs both domestically and internationally with companies trying to obtain competitor's trade secrets. In 2015, the FBI stated that just in the past year there has been a 53% increase "in economic espionage cases, or the theft of trade secrets leading to the loss of hundreds of billions of dollars."[63]

Infiltration of businesses to steal trade secrets is not a new concept but one that has evolved over time. Corporate espionage can take on many different forms and can include anything from smuggling, using spies to infiltrate a business, stealing employees, or hacking into corporate networks. One of the more famous cases of corporate espionage can be found dating all the way back to the early 1700s. Pere d'Entrecolles was a French Jesuit missionary and while in China "he learned the secret techniques for manufacturing [porcelain]."[64] He accomplished this by "gaining access to the kilns, studying Chinese books," and gaining intelligence from those who made porcelain.[65] He sent these stolen secrets to France through letters.[66] This theft of trade secrets was borne out of D'Entrecolles curiosity and not because he was paid by France or a corporation.[67]

While D'Entrecolles did not set out to become an industrial spy, employees from many companies have either turned rogue or been bought to reveal competitor's trade secrets. For example, "in 1993 General Motors (GM) accused Volkswagen of industrial espionage."[68] General Motors claimed its corporate secrets were used at Volkswagen after Jose Ignaclo Lopez, General Motors Opel division chief of production, and seven other executives left and went to work for Volkswagen.[69] General Motors and Volkswagen eventually reached a settlement, with General Motors agreeing to drop its lawsuit in exchange for Volkswagen's pledge to buy one billion dollars' worth of General Motors parts over seven years in an addition to paying General Motors 100 million dollars."[70]

---

[62] *Industrial Espionage*, The Free Dictionary, http://www.thefreedictionary.com/Corporate+espionage (last visited Jan. 8, 2017).
[63] Carolyn Schrader, *Cyber Economic Espionage Impacts Businesses*, CYBER EXPERTS BLOG AT NATIONAL CYBERSECURITY INSTITUTE (Aug. 3, 2015) http://www.nationalcybersecurityinstitute.org/general-public-interests/cyber-economic-espionage-impacts-businesses/.
[64] Famous Cases of Corporate Espionage, BLOOMBERG, https://www.bloomberg.com/news/photo-essays/2011-09-20/famous-cases-of-corporate-espionage (last visited Jan. 8, 2017).
[65] *Id.*
[66] *Id.*
[67] *Id.*
[68] *Id.*
[69] *Id.*
[70] Famous Cases of Corporate Espionage, BLOOMBERG, https://www.bloomberg.com/news/photo-essays/2011-09-20/famous-cases-of-corporate-espionage (last visited Jan. 8, 2017).

Some of the latest attacks on corporations have been done remotely through computer hacking. In January 2010, Google disclosed that a cyberattack originating from China occurred resulting in the theft of Google's intellectual property.[71] Google was not the only company targeted through this cyberattack. Other companies operating in the areas of finance, technology, media, and chemical industries were also under cyberattack.[72]

The United States is repeatedly targeted for the theft of trade secrets. From 1998 to 2003, Silicon Valley alone has been targeted by at least 20 foreign nations for theft of trade secrets.[73] South Korea is not an exception when it comes to corporate espionage aimed at the United States.

---

[71] *Id.*
[72] *Id.*
[73] Edward Iwata, *More U.S. Trade Secrets Walk Out the Door with Foreign Spies*, USA TODAY (Feb. 13, 2003, 10:07 AM), http://usatoday30.usatoday.com/tech/news/2003-02-12-espionage_x.htm.

1. *Corporate espionage cases involving trade secrets between the United States and South Korea*

The most recent known act of corporate espionage between the United States and South Korea was uncovered in 2009. In 2009, DuPont,[74] a United States corporation, filed a civil trade secrets case against South Korean corporation, Kolon Industries Inc.,[75] for theft of its' trade secrets. Dupont Inc. has been around in one form or another for over two centuries[76] whereas Kolon Industries Inc. in its current capacity has only been around since 2010.[77]

In February of 2009, DuPont became aware that Kolon Industries had obtained DuPont's trade secrets and confidential information relating to DuPont's Kevlar aramid fiber.[78] "After two years of litigation, a September 2011 jury issued a verdict in favor of DuPont, finding Kolon liable for misappropriation of trade secrets."[79] On August 30, 2012, Justice Payne awarded "$919M in compensatory damages against Kolon, added an additional $350,000 in punitive damages, and enjoined Kolon from selling para-amid fiber products in the U.S. for twenty years."[80]

"The District Court also issued a permanent injunction against any further use or disclosure of DuPont trade secrets used in their Kevlar product.[81] Kolon filed an emergency motion to stay the injunction."[82] The Fourth Circuit granted the injunction.[83]

---

[74] According to DuPont's corporate website, E.I du Pont first established his business on July 19, 1802. He had studied advanced explosive techniques and used his knowledge and interest in these and other scientific exploration to produce product quality and manufacturing sophistication and efficiency. Today, DuPont has grown in to an industry that has a foothold in everything from agricultural products, food and personal care, high performance materials, industrial biotechnology, people and process safety, to finally polymers and fibers. DuPont might be best known more its Kevlar® fiber that goes into creating body armor. http://www.dupont.com/ (last visited Jan. 7, 2017).

[75] According to the Kolon Industries corporate website, Kolon Industries, Inc. first began operations in South Korea in 1957. Kolon Industries separated from the manufacturing department of Kolon Corporation and is now today its own separate independent company. Today, Kolon focuses on four major business divisions. These divisions are industrial materials, chemical, films/electronic materials, and fashion. Kolon has many overseas subsidiaries including two located in the United States with one being in Fairfield, New Jersey and the other being in Los Angeles, California. Overview, KOLON INDUSTRIES: COMPANY, http://www.kolonindustries.com/Eng//Company/company01_01.asp (last visited Jan. 7, 2017).

[76] DUPONT: OUR COMPANY, http://www.dupont.com/corporate-functions/our-company/dupont-history.html (last visited Jan. 7, 2017).

[77] KOLON INDUSTRIES, http://www.kolonindustries.com/Eng/index.asp (last visited Jan. 7, 2017).

[78] E.I. Dupont De Nemours & Co. v. Kolon Indus., 688 F. Supp. 2d 443, 447-448 (E.D. Va. 2009).

[79] *DuPont Inc. v. Kolon USA Inc*, BROOKLYN LAW SCHOOL: TRADE SECRETS INSTITUTE, http://tsi.brooklaw.edu/cases/dupont-inc-v-kolon-usa-inc, (last visited Feb. 11, 2017).

[80] *Id.*

[81] *Id.*

[82] *Id.*

[83] E.I. DuPont de Nemours & Co. v. Kolon Indus., 871 F. Supp. 2d 513 (E.D. Va. 2012).

Ultimately, the Fourth Circuit on April 3, 2014, overturned the jury verdict awarding DuPont significant damages.[84] The court stated that, "the district court abused its discretion, to Kolon's prejudice, when it granted one of DuPont's pre-trial motions in limine and thereby excluded evidence material to Kolon's defense."[85] "Kolon Industries Inc. eventually admitted to "conspiring to steal DuPont Co.'s Kevlar trade secrets as a U.S. judge signed off on its plea agreement and $360 million penalty. Kolon's penalty in the criminal case includes an $85 million fine and $275 million in restitution to DuPont."[86] Kolon also settled its related civil lawsuit in federal court where terms of that agreement were not disclosed.

In the aftermath of *DuPont Inc. v. Kolon USA Inc.*, many companies have pushed for tougher legislation to defend trade secrets. In response to cases of industrial espionage and outcries from many in the business world, Congress passed the Defend Trade Secrets Act of 2016.[87] This Act became public law on May 11, 2016.[88] "The Defend Trade Secrets Act of 2016 adds a civil component to the federal law making it a crime to steal intellectual property."[89] "The prosecution of Kolon was among at least 20 economic espionage and trade-secret cases the Justice Department brought against individuals and companies from 2009 to 2012."[90]

VII. IMPROPER SOLICITATION AND GRAFT ACT

A. Background to the Improper Solicitation and Graft Act

Many experiments have been done around the world to gauge honesty and integrity of different cultures. For example, "researchers at the University of East Anglia in the UK devised an experiment to test personal honesty in 15 countries."[91] The experiment was simple. Individuals were given a coin to toss privately and then reported the result.[92] "Participants were told they would get more money if heads came up more times than tails." The results of this experiment showed that South Korea came out low on the honesty scale.[93] Bribes are just one of many ways of being dishonest.

---

[84] E.I. Dupont De Nemours & Co. v. Kolon Indus., 564 F. App'x 710 (4th Cir. 2014).
[85] *Id.* at 710, 711.
[86] Andrew Zajac, *Kolon Guilty in Kevlar Secrets Case, Settles with DuPont*, BLOOMBERG TECHNOLOGY (Apr. 30, 2015 11:12 AM), https://www.bloomberg.com/news/articles/2015-04-30/kolon-pleads-guilty-in-360-million-deal-as-dupont-suit-settled.
[87] Defend Trade Secrets Act, 18 U.S.C. § 1 (2016). https://www.congress.gov/114/plaws/publ153/PLAW-114publ153.pdf.
[88] *Id.*
[89] Gregory Korte, *Obama Signs Trade Secrets Bill, Allowing Companies to Sue*, USA Today (May 11, 2016, 4:29 PM), http://www.usatoday.com/story/news/politics/2016/05/11/obama-signs-trade-secrets-bill-allowing-companies-sue/84244258/.
[90] Andrew Zajac, *Kolon Guilty in Kevlar Secrets Case, Settles with DuPont*, BLOOMBERG TECHNOLOGY (Apr. 30, 2015 11:12 AM), https://www.bloomberg.com/news/articles/2015-04-30/kolon-pleads-guilty-in-360-million-deal-as-dupont-suit-settled.
[91] *Why South Korea's Corruption Scandal is Nothing New*, BBC NEWS: ASIA, (Nov. 24, 2016), http://www.bbc.com/news/world-asia-38078039.
[92] *Id.*
[93] *Id.*

1. Bribery

Bribes are viewed differently across cultures. Western culture and East Asian culture view bribes differently. Many Asian cultures use gift giving in ways that Western cultures would view as bribes. In Asian cultures, "[g]ift-giving is seen as an act of reciprocity and often misconstrued as bribery by Westerners, yet it appears to be an important constituent of the Asian culture and can be seen as a form of relationship investment, that if cultivated well, can uplift interactions between businesses."[94] When it comes to gift giving customs and the significance placed on them in Asia, South Korea ranks second.[95]

"South Korea is a gift-giving society where tokens are constantly exchanged as signs of respect, appreciation or friendship."[96] Paying for meals, giving gifts, and gifting money are just some of the ways in which Koreans express themselves in their gift-giving society. However, "because cash and material objects are so generously given and routinely expected, too often the boundaries of gift-giving and bribery-giving become unclear."[97] Due to this culture, South Korea has previously enacted several pieces of legislation aimed at fighting bribery.

---

[94] Clare D' Souza, *An inference of gift-giving within Asian business culture*, Asia Pacific Journal of Marketing and Logistics, Vol 15 Iss ½ pp. 27-28 (2003). http://www.cmeraldinsight.com/doi/abs/10.1108/13555850310765051. According to their website, the Asia Pacific Journal of Marketing and Logistics (APJML) provides a unique focus on marketing and logistics in the Asia Pacific region. *Id.* The journal publishes research which focuses on marketing and logistics problems, new procedures and practical approaches, systematic and critical reviews of changes in marketing and logistics and cross-national and cross-cultural comparisons of theory into practice. *Id.* Dr. Clare D'Souza is an associate professor in the college of Arts, Social Sciences and Commerce at the La Trobe Business School in Melbourne.*Id.* According to La Trobe Business School's staff website, Dr. D'Souza comes from a multi-disciplinary background and has been an academic for over ten years. http://www.latrobe.edu.au/law/staff/profile?uname=cmdsouza. She has taught a range of subjects from Entrepreneurship to Consumer Behavior to International Marketing. *Id.* Dr. D'Souza has taught in several countries of Asia and Europe. *Id.* She has also served as a strategic consultant for many international organization and has advised private and government agencies in both Australia and overseas. *Id.*
[95] David James, *Gift Giving Customs in Asia*, BSI CORPORATION, http://www.bsicorp.net/articles/keys-to-success/gift-giving-customs-asia (last visited Jan. 22, 2017). According to its website, Business Strategies International (BSI) is a San-Francisco based consulting and venture development firm that helps businesses (Asian or Western) successfully find markets and investments, select partners and representatives, establish join ventures and strategic alliances, and set up operations in the United States and Asia-Pacific countries. http://www.bsicorp.net/. David James is president of Business Strategies International. *Id.* He has served as an executive of three international corporations: Dillingham Corporation, Crown Zellerbach Corporation, and Texasgulf Inc. *Id.* He graduated from Harvard University, the University of Chicago Law School, and Stanford Business School's Executive Program. *Id.*
[96] David I. Steinberg, *Gift Giving and Politics in South Korea*, THE WALL STREET JOURNAL, (Sept. 12, 1996, 12:01 AM), http://www.wsj.com/articles/SB842462563700193500.
[97] Jon Huer, *Gift-Giving and Bribery Culture in Korea*, THE KOREA TIMES, (Aug 23, 2009, 10:54 PM), http://www.koreatimes.co.kr/www/news/opinon/2010/03/137_50572.html.

In 1998, South Korea passed the Act on Combating Bribery of Foreign Public Officials in International Business Transaction or more commonly known as the Foreign Bribery Prevention Act (FBPA) which "was passed to implement the Organization for Economic Cooperation and Development's (OECD) Convention on Combating Bribery of Foreign Public Officials in International Business Transactions." [98] Under the Foreign Bribery Prevention Act (the FBPA), "anyone who promises, gives or offers a bribe to a foreign public official in relation to his/her official business to obtain an improper advantage in international business transaction is subject to up to 5 years imprisonment or a fine up to KRW 20 million[99]."[100]

When it comes to bribery, "the text of the FBPA only requires the bribe to be done for the purpose of obtaining an improper advantage in international business transactions."[101] Even with the implementation of laws such as the Foreign Bribery Prevention Act, many scandals have occurred both domestically and internationally. In fact, many scandals that occur in South Korea are related to bribes.

---

[98] Mark S. Cohen, Jonathan S. Abernethy, and Soeun Nikole Lee, *Anti-Corruption Enforcement in Korea: IS an Old Law Coming of Age?*, NEW YORK LAW JOURNAL, (Nov. 4, 2013), https://www.cohengresser.com/assets/publications/11-4-2013_Anti-Corruption_Enforcement_in_Korea.pdf.

[99] 20 million KRW is approximately $17,893.73 USD http://www.xe.com/currencyconverter/convert/?Amount=20%2C000%2C000&From=KRW&To=USD (last visited April. 1, 2017).

[100] Kurt Gerstner and Hyunah Kim, *The FBPA: South Korea's Act to prevent bribery of foreign officials*, LEE INTERNATIONAL, (2010),http://www.inhousecommunity.com/wp-content/uploads/2016/07/v11i10_jur_SK.pdf.

[101] Mark S. Cohen, Jonathan S. Abernethy, and Soeun Nikole Lee, *Anti-Corruption Enforcement in Korea: IS an Old Law Coming of Age?*, NEW YORK LAW JOURNAL, (Nov. 4, 2013), https://www.cohengresser.com/assets/publications/11-4-2013_Anti-Corruption_Enforcement_in_Korea.pdf.

South Korea has continuously been in the news over the past decade for scandals occurring everywhere from the business sector to the government. Some of the scandals that the international community has picked up on include scandals involving Korean Airlines[102], Hyundai[103], Samsung[104], Hanjin Shipping[105], Lotte Duty Free[106], the Sewol ferry accident[107], and the ongoing impeachment of the current South Korean President Park

---

[102] In December of 2014, Heather Cho made international headlines after she ordered a plane to be turned back to the gate at JFK airport in New York. CNN reported that Cho ordered the plane to be turned back to relieve a flight attendant of duty after she was served nuts in a bag instead of on a plate. Laura Smith-Spark, *Korean Air Executive Resigns Over Nuts on a Plate Row*, CNN (Dec. 9, 2014, 9:45 AM), http://www.cnn.com/2014/12/09/world/asia/korean-air-nuts-scandal/index.html. Cho at the time was not only the vice president of Korean Air but also the eldest daughter to Korean Air's chairman. *Id.* She was not serving in an official capacity on that flight. *Id.*

[103] In 2006, South Korea indicted Chung Mong-koo, chairman of Hyundai Motor Company. Chung was at the time suspected of embezzling company funds to create a slush fund. According to Fox News, prosecutors at the time suspected Chung of embezzling around $106 million dollars of company money to create a slush fund. Associated Press, *Hyundai Motor Chairman Arrested in Scandal*, FOX NEWS (Apr. 28, 2006), http://www.foxnews.com/story/2006/04/28/hyundai-motor-chairman-arrested-in-scandal.html.

[104] In connection with the impeachment of South Korea's President Park Geun-Hye, an arrest warrant was issued Monday, January 16, 2017, for Lee Jae-Yong, Samsung Electronics vice chairman. Associated Press, *South Korea Seeks Arrest of Samsung Heir as Bribery Suspect in Political Scandal*, FOX NEWS, (Jan. 16, 2017), http://www.foxnews.com/world/2017/01/16/south-korea-seeks-arrest-samsung-heir-as-bribery-suspect-in-political-scandal.html. The vice chairman is facing allegations of both embezzlement and lying under oath as well as offering bribes. Id. Lee is suspected of giving 43 billion won, around 36 million in U.S. dollars, to Choi Soon-sil in an attempt to have the government help him with a leadership succession within Samsung. *Id.*

[105] Hanjin Shipping is not only South Korea's largest shipping group, but it is the world's seventh largest. Hanjin has encountered financial difficulties and is close to filing for bankruptcy. Prosecutors in South Korea are investigating Choi Eun-Young, the former chairwoman of Hanjin Shipping, for selling off shares in the company the day before Hanjin's prices crashed and news was published concerning Hanjin's financial difficulties. Stephen Evans, *Hanjin Bankruptcy: Are South Korea's 'Chaebols' in Crisis?*, BBC NEWS, (Sept. 8, 2016), http://www.bbc.com/news/business-37295185.

[106] Lotte Duty Free is a leader in duty free shopping. In 2015, they were ranked third in the world among duty free stores. LOTTE DUTY FREE, http://en.lottedfs.com/about/lottedfs. The vice chairman was found dead in late August of 2016 after committing suicide hours before he was supposed to be questioned by prosecutors. The prosecution team had raided Lotte offices back in June 2016 looking for a slush fund as well as for a breach of trust involving transactions among the group's companies. Business News, *Lotte Vice Chairman Found Dead Amid Probe; Suicide Suspected*, REUTERS, (Aug. 26, 2016, 8:30 AM), http://www.reuters.com/article/us-lottegroup-executive-idUSKCN11102Z.

[107] On April 16, 2014, the Sewol ferry carrying hundreds of high school students sank. Madison Park and Paula Hancocks, *Sewol ferry disaster: One year on, grieving families demand answers*, CNN (Apr. 16, 2015, 12:38 AM), http://www.cnn.com/2015/04/15/asia/sewol-ferry-korea-anniversary/. The crew instructed passengers to remain in place. Id. The ferry was carrying 476 people, and resulted in the loss of 304 lives, 250 of whom were high school students. Daniel Peters, *The classroom frozen in time: Eerie pictures of student desks untouched since they drowned in South Korean ferry disaster two years ago*, DAILY MAIL: News, (May 24, 2016, 12:48 AM), http://www.dailymail.co.uk/news/article-3605976/Eerie-pictures-untouched-classroom-belonging-students-teachers-killed-Sewol-ferry-disaster-South-Korea.html. Sewol's captain, Lee Joon-seok, who was widely derided for jumping to safety, was sentenced to 36 years in prison for abandonment causing death and injury, and violating sea laws. Madison Park and Paula Hancocks, *Sewol ferry disaster: One year on, grieving families demand answers*, CNN (Apr. 16, 2015, 12:38 AM), http://www.cnn.com/2015/04/15/asia/sewol-ferry-korea-anniversary/.

Geun-hye.[108] These scandals and corruption,[109] along with South Korea's battle against bribes, has led to the passing of the Improper Solicitation and Graft Act, also known as the Kim Young-ran Act, "after the former head of the Anti-corruption and Civil Rights Commission who led the preparation of the original bill."[110]

2. Kim Young-ran Act

The Improper Solicitation and Graft Act officially took effect on September 28, 2016, after Korea's Constitutional Court ruled that all the clauses of the Improper Solicitation and Graft Act were constitutional.[111] "The bill passed the review 870 days after the Anti-Corruption and Civil Rights Commission pre-announced the bill in August 2012, when Kim Young-ran served as chairman of the commission."[112]

---

[108] On December 9, 2016, President Park Geun-hye was impeached following protests. *South Korea President Park Geun-hye Impeached over Corruption Scandal*, CBS NEWS, (Dec. 9, 2016, 2:39 AM), http://www.cbsnews.com/news/south-korean-lawmakers-vote-to-impeach-president-park-geun-hye/. Then, the South Korean National Assembly voted 236 to 56 to impeach President Park. *Id.* One of the issues of her impeachment comes from her friendship with Choi Soon-il, who is also President Park's informal adviser. James Griffiths, *South Korea Presidential Scandal: What you need to know*, CNN, (Dec. 9, 2016, 4:38 AM), http://www.cnn.com/2016/11/02/asia/south-korea-president-scandal-explained/index.html. South Korean prosecutors have taken Choi Soon-il into custody on charges of abuse of power and attempted fraud. *Id.* These come from allegations that she not only had access to secret government documents but also that she may have intervened in state affairs. *Id.*

[109] *See* Justin Fendos, *South Korea's Corruption Culture*, THE DIPLOMAT, (Nov. 17, 2016), http://thediplomat.com/2016/11/south-koreas-corruption-culture/ (detailing South Korea's tendency toward corruption and how it has shifted in recent years).

[110] Latham & Watkins LLP, *Expansive Korean Anti-Corruption Law Comes into Force*, LEXOLOGY, (Sept. 8, 2016), http://www.lexology.com/library/detail.aspx?g=5b8f7394-fa99-4db5-9dca-197314d36497. According to its website, Latham & Watkins's administrative officers are located across the globe and manage the full spectrum of services and operations. *Administration*, LATHAN & WATKINS LLP, https://www.lw.com/AboutUs/Administration (last visited Apr. 15, 2017). Lathan & Watkins specializes in many different areas of practice such as Banking, Corporate Governance, Export Controls, Economic Sanctions & Customs, Greater China Practice, Mergers and Acquisitions, and Korea Practice. *Practices*, LATHAN & WATKINS, https://www.lw.com/practices (last visited Apr. 15, 2017).

[111] Ser Myo-Ja, *Constitutional Court upholds antigraft law*, KOREA JOONGANG DAILY (Jul. 7, 2016), http://koreajoongangdaily.joins.com/news/article/article.aspx?aid=3021918.

[112] Yu Jeong-in & Bak Sun-bong, *The "Kim Young-ran Act," a Ban on Bribery and Solicitation: Lawmakers to Pass the Bill on January 12*, THE KYUNGHYAN SHINMUN (Sept. 1, 2015, 5:31 PM), http://english.khan.co.kr/khan_art_view.html?artid=201501091731107&code=710100. According to its website, the Kyunghyang Shinmun was founded in 1946 and the newspaper claims it is at the front line of investigating activities of the government and Chaebols (conglomerates). *About us*, KYUNGHYANG SHINMUN, http://www.khan.co.kr/aboutkh/engkh.html (last visited Apr. 15, 2017).

The purpose of the Act "is to ensure that public officials and relevant persons fulfill their duties uprightly and to secure public confidence in public institutions by forbidding improper solicitations to public officials and relevant persons and by prohibiting them from accepting financial or other advantages."[113] A spokesperson of a new compliance team state that the Act "imposes fines on those individuals who make improper solicitation to public officials, executive and staff members of public service-related organizations, journalists and officials of private education institutions, as well as public officials who do not report such requests."[114]

This law "also differs from any predecessor as it implements a principle of 'dual punishment', enabling authorities to penalise [sic] both the giver and receiver of bribes."[115] The Act has 15 different categories of what would be considered improper solicitations of public officials.[116] One category makes it improper to exert[] influence on any "authorization, permission, license, patent, approval, inspection, examination, test, certification, verification" related to application submission.[117] Another category involves mitigating or remitting various administrative dispositions or punishments such as taxes, charges, fines for negligence, or penalties.[118] The implementation of this new Act has led to many concerns and reactions among both the national and international community.

3. Concerns about the Kim Young-ran Act

The Korean government has estimated that the number of those who will be subject to this anti-corruption act will be as many as 3 million.[119] Analysts and citizens of South Korea are concerned that the act "will have a negative impact on the economy."[120] Many South Koreans fear that "the demand for luxury goods and services in department stores, upscale hotels, country clubs, and high-end restaurants" will take the brunt of the effects.[121]

---

[113] The Improper Solicitation and Graft Act, Act No. 13278, Mar. 27, 2015, art. 1 (S. Kor.), *translated in* Reliable Ministry of Government Legislation National Law Information Center, http://www.law.go.kr/eng/engLsSc.do?menuId=1&query=improper+solicitation+&x=24&y=29#liBgcolor0 (click on "The Improper Solicitation and Graft Act").

[114] Christ Thomson, *Corruption clampdown*, ASIAN LEGAL BUSINESS, http://www.legalbusinessonline.com/features/corruption-clampdown/73173 (Sept. 16, 2016).

[115] *Id.*

[116] The Improper Solicitation and Graft Act, Act No. 13278, Mar. 27, 2015, art. 5 (S. Kor.), *translated in* Reliable Ministry of Government Legislation National Law Information Center, http://www.law.go.kr/eng/engLsSc.do?menuId=1&query=improper+solicitation+&x=24&y=29#liBgcolor0 (click on "The Improper Solicitation and Graft Act").

[117] *Id.*

[118] *Id.*

[119] *Anti-corruption "Kim Young-ran Law" Passes the National Assembly*, KOREA IT TIMES (Mar. 5, 2015), http://koreaittimes.com/story/45888/anti-corruption-kim-young-ran-law-passes-national-assembly.

[120] *Id.*

[121] *Id.*

"The Act is expected to significantly impact business activities in Korea involving national and local governments, quasi-government institutions, public and private educational institutions, and media companies."[122] Specifically by:

> 1) expanding the definition of public officials and others subject to regulation; 2) prohibiting improper solicitations to public officials regardless of whether such improper solicitation is accomplished by an offer to pay or payment of money or a thing of value; 3) setting relatively low ceilings on gifts, entertainment or other valuables that can be provided to public officials, regardless of whether such payment was related to the public official's duties; and 4) extending the prohibition relating to gifts, entertainment or other valuables to the spouses of public officials if offered or provided in connection with the public official's duties.[123]

Civil servants[124] in Korea are also concerned about the enactment of the Kim Young-ran Act. Those who work as civil servants and accept more than one million won, which is approximately 900 US dollars are subject to punishment.[125] The Act specifically "forbids people from buying a meal worth more than 30,000 Korean won ($27) . . . It also limits gifts to $45, and donations to $90."[126] A violation of the Act "could result in up to three years of in prison and thousands of dollars in fine, and it is irrelevant whether the money was related to an official's duties or positions, or whether favors were given in return."[127]

Finally, small businesses have concerns. South Korea has a "traditional culture of giving gifts on anniversaries such as Teacher's day and Chinese New Year as well as giving cash at life events such as funerals and weddings."[128] South Korean traditional culture also includes "taking people in business relationships to meals."[129] According to "a spokesman for South Korea's Small Enterprise and Market Service reported CNN that estimated losses for small businesses, including small traders and business owners and those involved in agriculture and forestry amounts to $2.6 billion and a loss of 1.26 million customers." Overall, the publics' reactions to the Act have been mixed.

---

[122] Catherine E. Palmer et al., *Expansive Korean Anti-Corruption Law Comes into Force*, LATHAM & WATKINS, (Sept. 12, 2016), https://www.lw.com/thoughtLeadership/LW-korean-anti-corruption-law-comes-into-force.
[123] *Id.*
[124] Civil servants include positions such as teachers, both public and private, lawmakers, individuals working in the field of journalism and even their spouses. Sou Hee Sophie Yang, *South Korea's New Anti-corruption Law, Kim Young-ran Act, will Have a Significant Impact on Korean Economy*, COLUMBIA BUSINESS LAW REVIEW (Oct. 23, 2016, 4:11 PM) http://cblr.columbia.edu/archives/13976.
[125] *Id.*
[126] *Id.*
[127] *Id.*
[128] *Id.*
[129] *Id.*

4. Reactions to the Kim Young-ran Act

A recent poll conducted by Gallop Korea[130] in South Korea showed that "of those who oppose the law, 21% cited that "it will negatively impact the economy and dampen consumer sentiment."[131] Even though the law may have wide spread effects and 21% of the citizens oppose, "the same opinion poll found that 71% of South Koreans support a controversial new law that strictly controls the wining and dining of civil servants and public officials".[132] The poll further showed that "many South Koreans think the law may have negative short term impact but will eventually help point society in the right direction."[133]

After the National Assembly passed the Kim Young-ran Act, "the Korean Bar Association, the Journalists Association of Korea, representatives of Internet media, private schools and kindergartens filed petitions."[134] Those who filed petitions were concerned over whether the law would apply to "journalists and private school workers since they are not civil servants."[135] The Korean Supreme Court has "held the new act constitutional, rejecting all petitions challenging its scope and vagueness."[136]

5. Future of US businesses working with South Korea

With all of the corruption and scandals being revealed in South Korea, the Kim Young-ran Act adds another layer of protection for not only businesses in South Korea but businesses all over the world. Pressure from within South Korea may be key to transforming Korea's culture of gift-giving and bribes. The Kim Young-ran Act takes a stab at the very heart of this traditional culture. With this law aimed at curbing corruption from the bottom up, all level of employees should be put on alert that corruption is going to be dealt with in a swift and harsh manner.

---

[130] According to its website, Gallup Korea is a specialized research company with the greatest number of interviews, the highest brand awareness and them most frequently quoted by the press. GALLUP KOREA, http://www.gallup.co.kr/english/social.asp (last visited Aug. 15, 2017).
[131] Kenichi Yamada, *71% of South Koreans support anti-graft law*, NIKKEI: ASIAN REVIEW (Oct. 9, 2016, 2:00 AM), http://asia.nikkei.com/Politics-Economy/Policy-Politics/71-of-South-Koreans-support-anti-graft-law. According to Nikkei Asian Review's website, it has 24 bureaus across Asia and 1,300 local and international reporters. The Nikkei Asian Review states it is the only global publication with a uniquely Asian perspective, and its information hub gives readers access to detailed information on over 300 of Asia' leading companies. NIKKEI ASIAN REVIEW, http://asia.nikkei.com/info/about (last visited Aug. 15, 2017).
[132] *Id.*
[133] *Id.*
[134] *Constitutional Court upholds antigraft law*, KOREA JOONGANG DAILY (Jul. 7, 2016), http://koreajoongangdaily.joins.com/news/article/article.aspx?aid=3021918.
[135] *Id.*
[136] Sou Hee Sophie Yang, *South Korea's New Anti-corruption Law, Kim Young-ran Act, will Have a Significant Impact on Korean Economy*, COLUMBIA BUSINESS LAW REVIEW (Oct. 23, 2016, 4:11 PM) http://cblr.columbia.edu/archives/13976.

Businesses working with South Korea should be prepared to adapt to the Act. This can be done by assessing "compliance policies and programs to ensure conformity with the act."[137] Also, businesses should be aware that "a violation of the Act, or an investigation into a possible violation of the Act, may trigger an FCPA[138] investigation."[139] US businesses can add this Act to their arsenal to protect against theft of trade secrets. When working with Korean businesses or receiving Korean visitors, US businesses can keep this law in the back of their minds and use it to either sniff out potential spies or use it as a gentle reminder that they are aware of how the course of business should be conducted.

VIII. Conclusion

After having lived abroad in Asia for more than three years, it is easy to see the many cultural differences between Western and Eastern cultures. One such difference is our perceptions of bribery. Bribes play a role when it comes to doing business in Eastern cultures. The United States has been at the forefront of pushing forward legislation both nationally and internationally in an effort to punish those in the business realm of accepting or giving bribes. Bribery has led to cases of industrial espionage. Scandals found in all corners of South Korea have led for a push to deal with corruption and bribery. The result was the implementation of the Improper Solicitation and Graft Act also known as the Kim Young-ran Act. This Act attempts to curb bribery and corruption from the bottom up. While many in South Korea fear the repercussions on the economy that this Act may bring, many South Koreans are hoping that stability will follow and that South Korea may soon move up in ranks on the bribery scale.

---

[137] https://www.lw.com/thoughtLeadership/LW-korean-anti-corruption-law-comes-into-force, *supra* note 120.
[138] According the U.S. Securities and Exchange Commission website, the Foreign Corrupt Practices Act (FCPA), which was enacted in 1977, generally prohibits the payment of bribes to foreign officials to assist in obtaining or retaining businesses. *Foreign Corrupt Practices Act*, U.S. SECURITIES AND EXCHANGE COMMISSION https://www.sec.gov/spotlight/foreign-corrupt-practices-act.shtml (last visited Aug. 15, 2017). The SEC website further explains that the FCPA can apply to prohibited conduct anywhere in the world and extends to publicly traded companies and their officers, directors, employees, stockholders, and agents. *Id.*
[139] https://www.lw.com/thoughtLeadership/LW-korean-anti-corruption-law-comes-into-force, *supra* note 120.

CYBERSECURITY IN THE MARINE TRANSPORTATION SECTOR: PROTECTING INTELLECTUAL PROPERTY TO KEEP OUR PORTS, FACILITIES, AND VESSELS SAFE FROM CYBER THREATS
BY RACHEL FOOTE[1]

I. INTRODUCTION AND BACKGROUND 232
   A. The Importance of Marine Transportation 234
   B. The Necessity of Integrated Systems in the Maritime Industry 237
   C. The Gravity of the Cyber Threat 238
II. CURRENT GOVERNMENT REGULATIONS AND APPROACHES 239
   A. Marine Transportation 239
      1. Maritime Transportation Security Act of 2002 240
      2. Port Security Grant Program 242
   B. Critical Infrastructure 243
      1. Executive Order 13636 and Presidential Policy Directive 21 244
      2. National Institute of Standards and Technology Cybersecurity Framework 245
      3. United States Coast Guard Cyber Strategy 247
   C. Recent Cybersecurity Legislation 248
      1. 2014 Cybersecurity Legislation 248
         a. National Cybersecurity Protection Act of 2014 249
         b. Cybersecurity Enhancement Act of 2014 250
      2. Cybersecurity Act of 2015 and Recent Presidential Policy 251
         a. Cybersecurity Act of 2015 251
         b. 2016 Presidential Policy 252
III. MARITIME INDUSTRY PRACTICE AND GUIDANCE 255
   A. Baltic and International Maritime Council: The Guidelines on
      Cyber Security Onboard Ships 255
   B. International Maritime Organization: Interim Guidelines on
      Maritime Cyber Risk Management 258
   C. American Bureau of Shipping Guidance Notes 259
IV. RECOMMENDATIONS 262
   A. Create a Culture of Cyber Risk Awareness 262
   B. Ensure MTSA Required Plans Address Cyber Risk 262
   C. Develop Additional Maritime Focused Cybersecurity Legislation 263
V. CONCLUSION 264

---

[1] Rachel Foote is a part-time Juris Doctor candidate at Mitchell Hamline School of Law, expected to graduate in 2019. She is also an active duty member of the U.S. Coast Guard. The views presented in this article are those of the author alone and do not represent the views of the Coast Guard. The author would like to thank Professor Sharon Sandeen and the entire Cybaris editorial board for their feedback and support.

I. Introduction and Background

In the time of wooden sailing ships and docks, the tide, currents, and available manpower were the forces that had the most profound effect on marine transportation.[2] Today, ships, ports, and facilities are run by sophisticated computers and software systems. These systems control, among other things, vessel engines,[3] navigation,[4] and facility automation.[5] While many of these systems are covered by patents[6] and involve trade secrets,[7] they remain vulnerable to cyber-attacks because of their increasingly integrated nature. Indeed, depending on the target and level of severity, a cyber-attack could cause serious economic[8] and environmental impacts. For example, the Exxon Valdez grounding, which caused one of the largest oil spills in U.S. history, involved a release of 257,000 barrels of oil from a total of 1.2 million barrels that the vessel was carrying.[9] For comparison, modern crude oil carriers can carry up to 2.2 million barrels of crude oil.[10] A cyber-attack that successfully disrupted a crude carrier's navigation or steering, resulting in the vessel grounding, could cause an oil spill much more devastating than Exxon Valdez.

---

[2] Chris Oxlade, *History of Sailing Ships*, Q-FILES, https://www.q-files.com/technology/ships-and-boats/history-of-sailing-ships/ (last visited Nov. 8, 2016).
[3] *Automation and Marine Software*, ABB, http://new.abb.com/marine/systems-and-solutions/automation-and-marinesoftware (last visited Nov. 11, 2016) (ABB is an industrial technology company that sells marine software for monitoring and automation on vessels).
[4] TALK OF THE NATION: SCIENCE FRIDAY, HOW LARGE SHIPS USE NAVIGATION SYSTEMS (Nat'l Pub. Radio Jan. 20, 2012). http://www.npr.org/2012/01/20/145525012/how-large-ships-use-navigation-systems.
[5] U.S. GOV'T ACCOUNTABILITY OFFICE GAO-14-459, MARITIME CRITICAL INFRASTRUCTURE PROTECTION: DHS NEEDS TO BETTER ADDRESS PORT CYBERSECURITY 4 (2014) ("maritime stakeholders rely on numerous types of information and communications technologies to manage the movement of cargo throughout ports.").
[6] *Cf.* Press Release, ABB, ABB Again Heads List for Most Patent Applications Filed by a Swiss-based Company (Feb. 26, 2015), http://www.abb.com/cawp/seitp202/67a510c11e3e4656c1257df7005309a2.aspx (last visited Feb. 3, 2017).
[7] *See, e.g.*, L-3 Comm. Westwood Corp. v. Robichaux, No. 06-279, 2008 WL 577560 (E.D. La. Feb. 29, 2008).
[8] Matthew Chambers & Mindy Liu, *Maritime Trade and Transportation by the Numbers*, U.S. DEP'T OF TRANSP., http://www.rita.dot.gov/bts/sites/rita.dot.gov.bts/files/publications/by_the_numbers/maritime_trade_and_transportation/index.html (last visited Oct. 22, 2016) (according to 2011 data, 53% of U.S. import value and 38% of U.S. export value was by vessel, the largest share of any mode of transportation); Lily Hay Newman, *What if a Cybersecurity Attack Shut Down Our Ports?*, SLATE (May 11 2015, 11:16 AM), http://www.slate.com/articles/technology/future_tense/2015/05/maritime_cybersecurity_ports_are_unsecured.html (last visited Nov. 11 2016) ("90 percent of the world's goods are shipped on boats.").
[9] *Oil Spill Facts: Questions and Answers About the Spill*, EXXON VALDEZ OIL SPILL TRUSTEE COUNCIL, http://www.evostc.state.ak.us/%3FFA=facts.QA (last visited Nov. 1, 2016).

[10] *Today in Energy: September 16, 2014*, U.S. ENERGY INFO. ADMIN., http://www.eia.gov/todayinenergy/detail.php?id=17991 (last visited Oct. 22, 2016) (very large crude carriers are responsible for most global crude oil shipments, and carry between 1.9 million and 2.2 million barrels of crude oil).

This significant and developing threat to the marine transportation sector has been the subject of comparatively little regulation and guidance. While parts of the Maritime Transportation and Security Act of 2002 (MTSA) can be read to include cyber vulnerabilities, the Act was not originally written with this threat in mind.[11] In February 2016, the Baltic and International Maritime Council (BIMCO) and several other influential maritime associations released "The Guidelines on Cyber Security Onboard Ships."[12] The International Maritime Organization (IMO) followed suit in June 2016, releasing interim guidelines addressing cyber risk.[13] Additionally, the American Bureau of Shipping (ABS) released a series of volumes addressing cybersecurity for marine and offshore facilities, the first published in February 2016.[14]

Given that maritime cybersecurity is a relatively new area of emphasis, this Note will look to develop a foundation from which to build future research and recommendations. This Note will first provide an overview of the maritime industry and highlight industry reliance on integrated systems. Section II will survey current United States government regulations and approaches, including methods found in the critical infrastructure sector. Section III will examine the recently promulgated industry guidance. From this data, this Note will posit some basic procedural, regulatory, and legislative suggestions to assist the maritime industry in continuing to protect its critical intellectual property and to ensure the safety of vessels and United States ports.

---

[11] Maritime Transportation Security Act of 2002, Pub. L. No. 107-295, 116 Stat. 2064 (2002) ("An Act To amend the Merchant Marine Act, 1936, to establish a program to ensure greater security for United States seaports, and for other purposes.").
[12] BALTIC & INT'L MAR. COUNCIL, *infra* note 224.
[13] INT'L MAR. ORG., *infra* note 251.

A. *The Importance of Marine Transportation*

According to findings for the 2002 Maritime Transportation and Security Act, the United States has 361 public ports.[15] Maritime ports in the U.S. handle over $1.3 trillion in cargo annually.[16] A significant disruption of the marine transportation sector would cause severe economic complications, especially if it impacted one of our top twenty-five ports.[17] Ports and port facilities are vulnerable to cyber-attacks because they rely on communications and information technologies to achieve cargo movement within the port.[18] These systems include terminal operating systems, industrial control systems, business operations systems, and access control and monitoring systems.[19] In 2014, "a major U.S. port facility suffered a system disruption which shut down multiple ship-to-shore cranes for several hours."[20] Protection of Maritime Critical Infrastructure[21] is crucial for American prosperity and security. A cyber-attack at a port could have a ripple effect that impacts other critical infrastructure sectors.[22]

Marine transportation is not specifically called out as one of the sixteen critical infrastructure sectors[23] identified in Presidential Policy Directive Twenty-One, however, it can be considered a subset of the "Transportations Systems" sector.[24] All of the sectors rely, to a certain degree, on the goods that make their way through U.S. ports.[25] However, the sectors most likely to be significantly affected by a port disruption are Transportation Systems, Critical Manufacturing, Chemical, Energy, Food and Agriculture, and Commercial Facilities.[26]

---

[14] 1 AMERICAN BUREAU OF SHIPPING, *infra* note 264.
[15] Maritime Transportation Security Act § 101(1) (2002).
[16] U.S. GOV'T ACCOUNTABILITY OFFICE, *supra* note 4 at 1.
[17] Maritime Transportation Security Act § 101(5) ("Twenty-five United States ports account for 98 percent of all container shipments.").
[18] U.S. GOV'T ACCOUNTABILITY OFFICE, *supra* note 4 at 4.
[19] *Id.* at 4–5.
[20] U.S. COAST GUARD, CYBER STRATEGY 17 (2015), https://www.uscg.mil/seniorleadership/DOCS/cyber.pdf.
[21] *Id.* at 31 ("Maritime Critical Infrastructure includes the ports, facilities, vessels, and related systems that facilitate trade within the U.S., support national defense and homeland security objectives, and connect the Nation to the global supply chain.").
[22] OFFICE OF CYBER & INFRASTRUCTURE ANALYSIS, CONSEQUENCES TO SEAPORT OPERATIONS FROM MALICIOUS CYBER ACTIVITY 12-16 (March 3, 2016, 13:00 EST), https://public.intelligence.net/dns-seaport-cyber-attacks.
[23] The White House, Presidential Policy Directive/PPD-21, Critical Infrastructure Security and Resilience (Feb. 12, 2013), https://www.whitehouse.gov/the-press-office/2013/02/12/presidential-policy-directive-critical-infrastructure-security-and-resil (the sectors are: Chemical, Commercial Facilities, Communications, Critical Manufacturing, Dams, Defense Industrial Base, Emergency Services, Energy, Financial Services, Food and Agriculture, Government Facilities, Healthcare and Public Health, Information Technology, Nuclear Reactors, Materials, and Waste, Transportation Systems, and Water and Wastewater Systems).
[24] *Id.*
[25] OFFICE OF CYBER & INFRASTRUCTURE ANALYSIS, *supra* note 21.
[26] *Id.*

A large number of industries included in the critical manufacturing sector are dependent "upon 'just-in-time' supply chains."[27] These industries can be significantly impacted by a disruption in port operations, leading to an interruption of the supply chain.[28] This could force companies within this sector to reduce or even halt production until port operations are normalized or another source of supply (not involving the impacted port(s)) is found.[29]

Another sector that relies on "just-in-time" supplies is the commercial facilities sector.[30] Companies in this sector keep limited inventory on hand, thus a port disruption could negatively impact business by disrupting the supply chain.[31] Indeed, it was projected that the West Coast ports labor slowdown in 2014–2015 "would cost the retail industry $7 billion in 2015 . . . due to missed sales, below optimal inventory levels, and the higher price of moving goods during the slowdown."[32]

The food and agriculture sector would also be negatively impacted by a maritime industry disruption.[33] In 2014, sixty-five percent of agricultural imports and seventy-three percent of exports were waterborne.[34] Temporary restrictions or closures of ports or waterways can increase product spoilage, leading to lost sales, and cause diversion to other transportation modes or ports, leading to higher transportation costs.[35] Additionally, a port disruption could lead to a shortage of products that are traditionally imported, such as sugar, coffee, and certain fruits and vegetables.[36]

---

[27] *Id.* at 12.
[28] *Id.*
[29] *Id.*
[30] OFFICE OF CYBER & INFRASTRUCTURE ANALYSIS, *supra* note 21 at 12.
[31] *Id.*
[32] *Id.* (*citing* Courtney Reagan, *West Coast Ports: Retail's $7 Billion Problem*, CNBC (Feb. 9, 2015, 12:58 PM), http://www.cnbc.com/2015/02/09/west-coast-ports-retails-7-billion-problem.html; Sarah Halzack, *Why a Major Backup at West Coast Ports Could Cost the Retail Industry Billions*, WASHINGTON POST (Feb. 17, 2015) https://www.washingtonpost.com/news/wonk/wp/2015/02/17/why-a-major-backup-at-west-coast-ports-could-cost-the-retail-industry-billions/.
[33] OFFICE OF CYBER & INFRASTRUCTURE ANALYSIS, *supra* note 21, at 13.
[34] Brian McGregor, *A Reliable Waterway System is Important to Agriculture*, U.S. DEP'T OF AGRIC., AGRIC. MKTG. SERV. 1 (Oct. 2015), https://www.ams.usda.gov/sites/default/files/media/Importance%20of%20Waterways%2010-2014.pdf.
[35] *Id.* at 7.
[36] OFFICE OF CYBER & INFRASTRUCTURE ANALYSIS, *supra* note 21, at 13.

The Energy Sector still relies on foreign oil imports—in 2015, petroleum imported from foreign countries constituted approximately twenty-four percent of petroleum consumption in the U.S.[37] This corresponded to about 9.4 million barrels per day.[38] In addition, the U.S. exported approximately 4.7 million barrels per day of petroleum to other countries.[39] In 2014, fifty-five percent of all daily petroleum imports into the U.S. were through maritime shipping.[40] A cyber-attack that disrupted crude oil imports could cause a temporary increase in the instability of gasoline prices and potentially cause regional shortages (depending on the length and scope of the disruption).[41] The Chemical Sector similarly relies on imports and exports.[42] A port disruption could cause increased prices and, if a significant disruption in the chemical supply chain occurs, production of manufactured chemicals could be hampered.[43]

Goods and products are regularly offloaded from ships and transferred to other modes of transportation such as rail and truck. Thus, the impact to the transportation sector would not only be an impact to maritime transport, but would likely also affect truck and rail transport.[44] Additionally, a major port disruption could cause impacted companies to ship their goods by air freight, possibly "caus[ing] congestion within the logistic chains of air freight companies, leading to delays in the movement of goods."[45] Shipping by air freight is typically more expensive, increasing costs for the businesses and potentially negatively impacting the economy.[46]

As discussed above, the maritime industry is critical to the prosperity of the United States. However, ships not only carry "the majority of freight arriving and departing from the U.S.," they move "the bulk of critical military cargoes around the globe."[47] Thus, a maritime disruption could present a grave risk to national security. In considering the critical role that marine transportation plays, the vulnerabilities of the interconnected systems that ports and vessels rely on must also be considered.

---

[37] *Frequently Asked Questions: How much oil consumed by the United States comes from foreign countries?*, U.S. ENERGY INFO. ADMIN., http://www.eia.gov/tools/faqs/faq.cfm?id=32&t=6 (last visited Dec. 21, 2016) ("Petroleum includes crude oil and petroleum products. Petroleum products include gasoline, diesel fuel, heating oil, jet fuel, chemical feedstocks, asphalt, biofuels (ethanol and biodiesel) and other products").
[38] *Frequently Asked Questions: How much petroleum does the United States import and export?*, U.S. ENERGY INFO. ADMIN., http://www.eia.gov/tools/faqs/faq.cfm?id=727&t=6 (last visited Dec. 21, 2016).
[39] *Id.*
[40] OFFICE OF CYBER & INFRASTRUCTURE ANALYSIS, *supra* note 21, at 14.
[41] *Id.*
[42] *Id.* at 16.
[43] *Id.*
[44] *Id.*
[45] *Id.*
[46] Tiffany Hsu, *Air Freight Firms are Bustling Amid Bottlenecks at West Coast Ports*, LA TIMES (Feb. 20, 2015, 2:19 PM), http://www.latimes.com/business/la-fi-air-cargo-20150221-story.html.
[47] WALLISCHECK, *infra* note 50 at 1.

B. The Necessity of Integrated Systems in the Maritime Industry

Vessels and ports rely heavily on information systems and communications to control security, communication, navigation, cargo movement and tracking, equipment operation, and business operations.[48] Given the emerging Internet of Things (IoT), and the fact that the original concept of IoT was to improve efficiency in manufacturing,[49] it is not surprising the that the maritime industry is using similar technology. Since the typical commercial vessel spends most of its time at sea, hardwired communications and human couriers are not available to carry information. Thus, a ship truly is a "thing" in IoT parlance[50]—a typical ship contains hundreds of sensors and systems that can be remotely accessed. Such industrial control systems (ICS) are truly pervasive—"[t]hey are aboard virtually [every] ship and in the shore-side infrastructure supporting them."[51] Many of these systems are integrated to improve vessel or port efficiency.[52] While not all systems are directly connected to the Internet, their inter-connected nature leaves them vulnerable.[53] Significantly, "[f]ailure of any one of these systems can produce cascading impacts in other systems and amplify the disruption to operations."[54]

Many ICS use commercial off-the-shelf technologies that are ripe for exploitation.[55] These systems are network-based and utilize widely available communication protocols and standard operating systems.[56] Additionally, many of these systems are Internet Protocol (IP) addressable.[57] This upsurge in the usage of IP addressable devices creates significant vulnerabilities, exponentially increasing the likelihood of a severe cyber-attack.[58]

---

[48] OFF. OF CYBER & INFRASTRUCTURE ANALYSIS, *supra* note 21 at 3.
[49] Robin Kester, Note, *Demystifying the Internet of Things: Industry Impact, Standardization Problems, and Legal Considerations*, 8 ELON L. REV. 205, 206 (2016).
[50] *See Id.*
[51] Eric York Wallischeck, *ICS Security in Maritime Transportation,*, JOHN A. VOLPE NATIONAL TRANSPORTATION SYSTEMS CENTER, 1 (2013), https://ntl.bts.gov/lib/48000/48000/48074/DOT-VNTSC-MARAD-13-01.pdf.
[52] OFF. OF CYBER & INFRASTRUCTURE ANALYSIS, *supra* note 21 at 7.
[53] "Even limited connection to the Internet exposes control systems to all of the inherent vulnerabilities of interconnected computer networks, including viruses, worms, hackers and terrorists." WALLISCHECK, *supra* note 50 at 12.
[54] OFF. OF CYBER & INFRASTRUCTURE ANALYSIS, *supra* note 21 at 7.
[55] WALLISCHECK, *supra* note 50 at 11.
[56] *Id.*
[57] *Id.* at 12.
[58] *Id.* at 9.

C. The Gravity of the Cyber Threat

In 2013, a research team from the University of Texas at Austin successfully used a GPS spoofing device to gain control of a ship's navigation system and subtly shift an $80 million yacht off its course.[59] The yacht was tricked onto a parallel course that was several hundred meters from its intended one.[60] While the Texas team was conducting the experiment in international waters, 30 miles offshore of Italy, an attack that shifted a vessel several hundred meters off course when it was closer to land or near navigation hazards could have serious consequences.[61] Unfortunately, this is not an isolated incident. Researchers have discovered potential vulnerabilities in all transportation modes (including maritime), involving a broad range of technologies.[62]

While the highly publicized Stuxnet attack in 2010 was not directed at the maritime industry, "it is important to recognize that the same techniques used in that incident could be used to disable comparable systems used worldwide . . . including the safe and reliable movement of cargo and passengers."[63] Thankfully, the marine transportation system has not suffered a significant cyber-attack. However, major disruptions to port operations can cause wide-ranging impacts to the American economy.[64] Commentators have stated that a "broad-based cyber-attack" on the marine transportation system that slowed or halted movement of cargo, could have significant economic impact.[65] "While a cyber-attack that disables a vessel transiting the Panama Canal may only affect a single waterway, it can have significant economic impact around the globe."[66] Thus, the significant threat presented by cyber-terrorism should not be ignored.

---

[59] Univ. of Tex. at Austin News, *UT Austin Researchers Successfully Spoof an $80 million Yacht at Sea* (July 29, 2013), http://news.utexas.edu/2013/07/29/ut-austin-researchers-successfully-spoof-an-80-million-yacht-at-sea.
[60] *Id.*
[61] *Id.*
[62] WALLISCHECK, *supra* note 50 at 2.
[63] *Id.* at 14.
[64] *See supra* Section I. A.
[65] WALLISCHECK, *supra* note 50 at 2.
[66] *Id.*

II. Current Governmental Regulations and Approaches

Cybersecurity is a topic that has gained significant awareness in the public consciousness.[67] Cyber-attacks are becoming more prominent and egregious in nature.[68] Much of the publicity has related to data breaches at major retailers[69] and banks,[70] but the maritime industry has occasionally gained the spotlight.[71] However, "the American public is generally unaware of . . . the impact that [Maritime Transportation System] disruptions pose to national security and economic stability. To most Americans, ships are floating hotels that travel to exotic ports . . . ."[72] This makes the risks to maritime transportation "often invisible" to the public.[73]

The United States government has continued to increase its focus on cybersecurity. President Obama recognized that "[c]yber incidents are a fact of contemporary life, and significant cyber incidents are occurring with increasing frequency, implicating public and private infrastructure located in the United States and abroad."[74] Current cybersecurity regulations and laws are piecemeal but are continuing to evolve.[75]

A. *Marine Transportation*

The principal laws that cover maritime security are the Maritime Transportation Security Act and the Security and Accountability for Every Port Act.

---

[67] Charles Beard et al, US Cybersecurity: Progress Stalled, Key Findings from the 2015 US State of Cybercrime Survey 4 (2015), http://www.pwc.com/us/en/increasing-it-effectiveness/publications/us-cybercrime-survey-2015.html (suggesting that "the term 'data breach' [has] become part of the broader public vernacular . . . .").
[68] *Id.*
[69] Michael Kassner, *Anatomy of the Target Data Breach: Missed opportunities and lessons learned*, ZDNet (Feb. 2, 2015, 8:29 AM), http://www.zdnet.com/article/anatomy-of-the-target-data-breach-missed-opportunities-and-lessons-learned/ (last visited Nov. 8, 2016).
[70] Portia Crowe, *JPMorgan Fell Victim to the Largest Theft of Customer Data from a Financial Institution in US History*, Business Insider (Nov. 10, 2015, 10:12 AM), http://www.businessinsider.com/jpmorgan-hacked-bank-breach-2015-11 (last visited Nov. 8, 2016).
[71] *See* Univ. of Tex. at Austin News, *supra* note 58.
[72] Wallischeck, *supra* note 50 at 2.
[73] *Id.*
[74] The White House, Presidential Policy Directive/PPD-41, United States Cyber Incident Coordination (July 26, 2016), https://www.whitehouse.gov/the-press-office/2016/07/26/presidential-policy-directive-united-states-cyber-incident.
[75] Chris Laughlin, Student Note, *Cybersecurity in Critical Infrastructure Sectors: A Proactive Approach to Ensure Inevitable Laws and Regulations are Effective*, 14 Colo. Tech. L.J. 345, 351 (2016).

1. *Maritime Transportation Security Act of 2002*

The Maritime Transportation Security Act (MTSA) was enacted in November 2002.[76] MTSA implements requirements for increased security in United States waterways, coastal areas, and ports.[77] The Act does not specifically address cybersecurity; however, it does require the development of Area Maritime Security (AMS) Plans, Vessel Security Plans, and Facility Security Plans.[78] These plans are designed to help ports, facilities, and vessels to prepare for and deter transportation security incidents.[79]

The Security and Accountability for Every Port Act (SAFE Port Act) was enacted in October 2006.[80] The Act is designed "[t]o improve maritime and cargo security through enhanced layered defenses . . . ."[81] The SAFE Port Act amended some MTSA provisions and also introduced new initiatives and programs. The latter included establishing a port security exercise program and directing the development of a strategic plan to enhance the security of the international supply chain.[82]

One critical aspect of MTSA was that it prompted the establishment of AMS Committees.[83] These committees have several key responsibilities, including identifying "critical port infrastructure and operations," identifying risks, and determining "mitigation strategies and implementation methods."[84] In addition, the committees are responsible for developing processes to continually evaluate security and assist in developing AMS Plans.[85] AMS Plans are based on the AMS Assessments that were directed by MTSA.[86]

---

[76] Maritime Transportation Security Act of 2002, Pub. L. No. 107-295, 116 Stat. 2064 (2002).
[77] *Id.*
[78] 46 U.S.C.A. § 70103 (2010).
[79] *Id.*; 46 U.S.C.A. § 70101(6) (2006) ("The term 'transportation security incident' means a security incident resulting in a significant loss of life, environmental damage, transportation system disruption, or economic disruption in a particular area.").
[80] Security and Accountability for Every Port Act of 2006, Pub. L. No. 109-347, 120 Stat. 1884 (2006).
[81] *Id.*
[82] 6 U.S.C.A. §§ 912, 941 (2016).
[83] 33 C.F.R. §§ 103.300, 103.305(a) (2016). "An AMS Committee will be composed of not less than seven members . . . who may be selected from—(1) The Federal, Territorial, or Tribal government; (2) The State government and political subdivisions thereof; (3) Local public safety, crisis management and emergency response agencies; (4) Law enforcement and security organizations; (5) Maritime industry, including labor; (6) Other port stakeholders having a special competence in maritime security; and (7) Port stakeholders affected by security practices and policies." *Id.* § 103.305(a).
[84] *Id.* § 103.310(a).
[85] *Id.* §103.310(a)(4).
[86] 46 U.S.C.A. § 70102(b) (2016) (stating that "the Secretary shall conduct a detailed vulnerability assessment of the facilities and vessels that may be involved in a transportation security incident."). These assessments shall be updated "at least every 5 years." *Id.* § 70102(b)(3). *See also* 33 C.F.R. §§ 103.400, 103.500.

AMS Assessments must: (1) identify critical port infrastructure and operations; (2) include a threat assessment identifying and evaluating potential threats; (3) include an assessment of consequences and vulnerabilities; and (4) make a security measures determination.[87] In meeting the specified elements, the assessment is to consider a number of variables including, but not limited to, physical security, security capabilities and resources, and "[r]adio and telecommunication systems, including computer systems and networks."[88] While the latter does not directly reference cybersecurity, it can be used to read the inclusion of cyber threats into MTSA. Furthermore, both Vessel Security Plans and Facility Security Plans required under MTSA must include information relating to communications and security systems.[89] Security plans must be updated every five years.[90]

A June 2014 report on maritime critical infrastructure by the Government Accountability Office (GAO) found that area maritime and facility security plans contained limited cybersecurity coverage.[91] The GAO attributed the limited coverage to the fact that the 2012 National Maritime Strategic Risk assessment developed by the Coast Guard did not address cyber risks in the maritime environment.[92] In testimony before the House Subcommittee on Border and Maritime Security, Gregory C. Wilshusen, Director of Information Security Issues for the GAO, noted that while the 2014 National Maritime Strategic Risk Assessment did identify cyber as a threat vector, it did not "fully address[] threats, vulnerabilities, and consequences of cyber incidents . . . ."[93] Director Wilshusen concluded that until this threat is more fully addressed, the "ability to appropriately plan and allocate resources for protecting maritime-related critical infrastructure" will be hindered.[94] The National Maritime Strategic Risk Assessment is conducted biennially,[95] with the next due in 2016.

---

[87] 33 C.F.R. § 103.405(a).
[88] *Id.* § 103.405(b)(5).
[89] *See id.* §§ 104.405, 105.405.
[90] 46 U.S.C.A. § 70103(c)(3)(G) (2016).
[91] *Maritime Critical Infrastructure Protection: DHS Needs to Better Address Port Cybersecurity, supra* note 4, at 16.
[92] *Id.* (the 2012 assessment was the most current available at the time of the report).
[93] *DHS Needs to Enhance Efforts to Address Port Cybersecurity: Hearing on Maritime Critical Infrastructure Protection Before the H. Subcomm. on Border and Maritime Security, H. Comm. on Homeland Security,* 114th Cong. 7 (2015) (statement of Gregory C. Wilshusen, Dir., Info. Security Issues, Gov't Accountability Off.).
[94] *Id.*
[95] *Id.* at 6.

2. Port Security Grant Program

MTSA also introduced the Port Security Grant Program (PSGP)[96] to help ports with funding for the security requirements it mandated.[97] The Federal Emergency Management Agency (FEMA) administers the program and consults with the U.S. Coast Guard, among others, to make award decisions.[98] The grant program was designed to allocate funds based on risk.[99]

The fiscal year (FY) 2014 PSGP Funding Opportunity Announcement (FOA) allowed applicants to request funding for cybersecurity vulnerability assessments.[100] Vulnerability assessments had not been something typically funded under PSGP; however, the FOA noted that "considering the relative newness of Cybersecurity as a priority within the program and the need to develop and enhance the voluntary Cybersecurity Framework, vulnerability assessments may be funded as contracted costs."[101] The FY 2014 PSGP also stated that cybersecurity was one of the funding focus areas.[102] FY 2014 was only the second year that cyber was considered a major funding priority.[103] Cybersecurity remained an identified funding priority in 2015 and 2016.[104]

---

[96] 46 U.S.C.A. § 70107 (2016).
[97] Commander Joseph Kramek, *The Critical Infrastructure Gap: U.S. Port Facilities and Cyber Vulnerabilities*, CTR. FOR 21ST CENTURY SEC. AND INTELLIGENCE 9 (July 2013), https://www.brookings.edu/wp-content/uploads/2016/06/03-cyber-port-security-kramek.pdf.
[98] *Id.*
[99] 46 U.S.C.A. § 70107(a) (2016) ("In administering the grant program, the Secretary shall take into account national economic, energy, and strategic defense concerns based upon the most current risk assessments available.").
[100] *Funding Opportunity Announcement: FY 2014 Port Security Grant Program*, FED. EMERGENCY MGMT. AGENCY 38 (2014), https://www.fema.gov/media-library-data/1396623742630-9e497a99bef3e3c0265bbf84993b5e69/FY_2014_PSGP_FOA_Final_Revised.pdf.
[101] *Id.*
[102] *FY 2014 Port Security Grant Program Fact Sheet*, FED. EMERGENCY MGMT. AGENCY 2 (2014), https://www.fema.gov/media-library-data/1406300857129-09e62587b8f79e748c585e37cdba09a9/PSGP_Fact%20Sheet_Final.pdf.
[103] Looking back as far as 2005, 2013 was the first year that cyber was specifically called out as a major funding priority. *See generally Port Security Grant Program*, FED. EMERGENCY MGMT. AGENCY, https://www.fema.gov/port-security-grant-program (last visited Mar. 27, 2017) (wherein FY 2005 data is the earliest available on the FEMA PSGP website).
[104] *FY 2015 Port Security Grant Program Fact Sheet*, FED. EMERGENCY MGMT. AGENCY 2 (2015), https://www.fema.gov/media-library-data/1438021685566-9cf51877eec3f17c6495b672334eb050/FY_2015_PSGP_Fact_Sheet_Allocations.pdf; *FY 2016 Port Security Grant Program Fact Sheet*, FED. EMERGENCY MGMT. AGENCY, 2 (2016), https://www.fema.gov/media-library-data/1467237017233-ba181560021a43339f4c3e0253212671/FY_2016_PSGP_Fact_Sheet_Final.pdf.

However, while cybersecurity was identified as a funding priority in 2014, the national review panel for grants did not reach out to any cyber subject matter experts to assist it in making decisions about which cyber-related grants were most worthy of funding.[105] For the 2015 grants, FEMA did report that "they have consulted with the Coast Guard's Cyber Command on high-dollar-value cyber projects and that Cyber Command officials sat on the review panel for one day to review several other cyber projects."[106] However, FEMA provided no formal written guidelines to ensure that grant reviewers consulted appropriate cyber expertise in either the field (captain of the port) level or national level review process.[107] The FY 2016 Notice of Funding Opportunity (NOFO) did contain a more detailed discussion of cybersecurity than previous years, however, it still did not require that grant reviewers consult cyber professionals when reviewing cyber projects.[108]

B. *Critical Infrastructure*

The National Infrastructure Protection Plan (NIPP) lays the foundation for private sector and government entities in the critical infrastructure community to work together to ensure critical infrastructure safety and resilience through proper risk management practices.[109] NIPP advocates an approach through public-private partnership, ensuring that all stakeholders in the critical infrastructure community are represented.[110] The 2013 NIPP update is consistent with Executive Order 13636, "Improving Critical Infrastructure Cybersecurity,"[111] and Presidential Policy Directive 21, "Critical Infrastructure Security and Resilience."[112]

---

[105] *DHS Needs to Enhance Efforts to Address Port Cybersecurity*, *supra* note 92, at 9.
[106] *Id.*
[107] *Id.*
[108] *Notice of Funding Opportunity: FY 2016 Port Security Grant Program*, FED. EMERGENCY MGMT. AGENCY 40 (2016), https://www.fema.gov/media-library-data/1455573875236-07ce03a778118ecc2ead8e1aae84185e/FY_2016_PSGP_NOFO_FINAL.pdf.
[109] *NIPP 2013: Partnering for Critical Infrastructure Security and Resilience*, U.S. DEP'T OF HOMELAND SEC. 1–2 (2013), https://www.dhs.gov/sites/default/files/publications/National-Infrastructure-Protection-Plan-2013-508.pdf.
[110] *Id.* at 3.
[111] Exec. Order No. 13,636, *infra* note 112.
[112] *NIPP 2013: Partnering for Critical Infrastructure Security and Resilience*, *supra* note 108; Presidential Policy Directive/PPD-21, *supra* note 22.

1. *Executive Order 13636 and Presidential Policy Directive 21*

In February 2013, President Obama signed Executive Order 13636, "Improving Critical Infrastructure Cybersecurity."[113] This order recognized that "[t]he cyber threat to critical infrastructure . . . represents one of the most serious national security challenges we must confront."[114] It defined critical infrastructure broadly: "systems and assets, whether physical or virtual, so vital to the United States that the incapacity or destruction of such systems and assets would have a debilitating impact on security, national economic security, national public health or safety, or any combination of those matters."[115] Arguably maritime critical infrastructure is covered under this definition.

Executive Order 13636 stated that "[i]t is the policy of the United States to enhance the security and resilience of the Nation's critical infrastructure and to maintain a cyber environment that encourages efficiency, innovation, and economic prosperity while promoting safety, security, business confidentiality, privacy, and civil liberties."[116] The Order promoted partnership between the government and the private sector, and sought to create an information sharing program that allowed for more timely sharing of information between the government and the private sector.[117] In addition, the Order directed all agencies to ensure that civil liberties and privacy protections were considered and incorporated into any cyber-related activities.[118]

On the same day that Executive Order 13636 was issued, President Obama also published Presidential Policy Directive Twenty-One (PPD-21), "Critical Infrastructure Security and Resilience."[119] The sixteen critical infrastructure sectors recognized by PPD-21 were each assigned a Federal Sector Specific Agency to lead the federal efforts.[120] PPD-21 focused on both the cyber and physical sides of critical infrastructure, and recognized the interconnected nature of infrastructure systems.[121]

---

[113] Exec. Order No. 13,636, 78 Fed. Reg. 11,739 (Feb. 12, 2013).
[114] *Id.* § 1.
[115] *Id.* § 2.
[116] *Id.* § 1.
[117] *Id.* § 4.
[118] *Id.* § 5.
[119] *Critical Infrastructure Security and Resilience, supra* note 22.
[120] *Id.* ("The term 'Sector-Specific Agency' (SSA) means the Federal department or agency designated under this directive to be responsible for providing institutional knowledge and specialized expertise . . . .").
[121] *Id.*

PPD-21 set three strategic imperatives to shape the Federal government approach.[122] The first imperative directs implementation of a "national unity of effort," designed to increase situational awareness and clarify relationships between public and private stakeholders.[123] The second imperative focuses on ensuring efficient information exchange, both within the government and with the operators and owners of critical infrastructure.[124] Like Executive Order 13636, PPD-21 stresses that information sharing "must be done while respecting privacy and civil liberties."[125] The final strategic imperative focuses on an "integration and analysis function," and seeks to use this function to inform both planning and operational decision making.[126]

2. *National Institute of Standards and Technology Cybersecurity Framework*

Executive Order 13636 also directed the National Institute of Standards and Technology (NIST) "to lead the development of a framework to reduce cyber risks to critical infrastructure."[127] The order directed that "[t]he Cybersecurity Framework shall include a set of standards, methodologies, procedures, and processes that align policy, business, and technological approaches to address cyber risks."[128]

The NIST Framework was promulgated on February 12, 2014, one year to the day after Executive Order 13636.[129] The Framework was collaboratively developed by both governmental and private sector entities and identified "a set of industry standards and best practices . . . ."[130] Use of the Framework is voluntary and it is designed to complement, rather than replace, existing processes and programs.[131] The Framework is broken down into "three parts: the Framework Core, the Framework Implementation Tiers, and the Framework Profiles."[132]

---

[122] *Id.*
[123] *Id.*
[124] *Critical Infrastructure Security and Resilience*, *supra* note 22. "(2) Enable effective information exchange by identifying baseline data and systems requirements for the Federal Government;..."
[125] *Id. see also*, Exec. Order No. 13636, *supra* note 112 at § 5(a).
[126] Presidential Policy Directive/PPD-21, *supra* note 22. NOTE: maybe use quote, "(3) Implement an integration and analysis function to inform planning and operations decisions regarding critical infrastructure."
[127] Exec. Order No. 13636, *supra* note 112, at § 7(a).
[128] *Id.*
[129] NAT'L INST. OF STANDARDS & TECH., FRAMEWORK FOR IMPROVING CRITICAL INFRASTRUCTURE CYBERSECURITY (2014), https://www.nist.gov/sites/default/files/documents/cyberframework/cybersecurity-framework-021214.pdf (last visited April 20, 2017).
[130] *Id.* at 1.
[131] *Id.* at 4.
[132] *Id.*

The Framework Core is based on five functions that are concurrent and should be continuously considered.[133] The functions are "Identify, Protect, Detect, Respond, [and] Recover,"[134] and are designed to represent a strategic, birds-eye ("high-level") view of cybersecurity risk.[135] The functions are further broken down into categories (functional groups)[136] and subcategories[137] (specific outcomes). In addition, informative references are given for each subcategory, capturing common practices used to achieve desired outcomes.[138]

The Framework Implementation Tiers are designed to reflect the level at which an entities' cybersecurity practices correspond to the risk management procedures described in the Framework.[139] The Tiers cover a range that moves from a more informal and reactive response, to responses that are adaptive and "risk-informed."[140] The Tiers help "provide context on how an organization views cybersecurity risk and the processes in place to manage that risk."[141] In order to determine the most appropriate Tier to mitigate risk and feasibly meet organizational goals, each organization should consider their unique constraints, objectives, threat environment, and legal or regulatory requirements.[142]

The Framework Profiles are the outcomes that organizations select from the Framework categories and subcategories based on their individual needs.[143] A Profile can be particularly helpful in examining an organization's current cybersecurity posture (i.e. "as is") and comparing it with a target Profile (i.e. hope "to be").[144] This comparison can help an organization identify steps that need to be taken to reach cybersecurity protection goals.[145] Organizations can have multiple Profiles, each aligned with particular cyber vulnerable business components and recognizing particular organizational needs.[146]

---

[133] *Id.*
[134] NAT'L INST. OF STANDARDS & TECH., FRAMEWORK FOR IMPROVING CRITICAL INFRASTRUCTURE CYBERSECURITY (2014), https://www.nist.gov/sites/default/files/documents/cyberframework/cybersecurity-framework-021214.pdf (last visited April 20, 2017).
[135] *Id.* at 4.
[136] *Id.* at 7, 19 (Figure 1 (p. 7) and Table 1 (p. 19)).
[137] *Id.* at 8. "Subcategories further divide a Category into specific outcomes of technical and/or management activities. They provide a set of results that, while not exhaustive, help support achievement of the outcomes in each Category."
[138] *Id.*
[139] NAT'L INST. OF STANDARDS & TECH., FRAMEWORK FOR IMPROVING CRITICAL INFRASTRUCTURE CYBERSECURITY 5 (2014), https://www.nist.gov/sites/default/files/documents/cyberframework/cybersecurity-framework-021214.pdf (last visited April 20, 2017).
[140] *Id.* at 5, 10 (the Tier definitions are: Tier 1 (Partial), Tier 2 (Risk Informed), Tier 3 (Repeatable), Tier 4 (Adaptive)).
[141] *Id.* at 9.
[142] *Id.*
[143] *Id.* at 5.
[144] NAT'L INST. OF STANDARDS & TECH., FRAMEWORK FOR IMPROVING CRITICAL INFRASTRUCTURE CYBERSECURITY 5 (2014), https://www.nist.gov/sites/default/files/documents/cyberframework/cybersecurity-framework-021214.pdf (last visited April 20, 2017).
[145] *Id.* at 11.
[146] *Id.*

The NIST Framework is a good starting point to strengthen cybersecurity programs. Additional standards developed collaboratively between the private sector and government should be encouraged. These additional standards could build on this initial Framework, adding to the depth and breadth of cybersecurity knowledge and showcasing best practices and procedures. Such additional collaborative products would benefit both the government and industry, helping maintain the security and resiliency of American critical infrastructure. The maritime industry has recognized the importance of the NIST Framework—all of the recently promulgated industry guidance cite the Framework and suggest incorporating many of its recommended practices.[147]

3. *United States Coast Guard Cyber Strategy*

Partially due to Executive Order 13636, the United States Coast Guard promulgated a Cyber Strategy in 2015.[148] This Strategy designates infrastructure protection as one of the Coast Guard's strategic priorities in the cyber domain.[149] It identifies two goals and four strategies to help address cyber risks to maritime critical infrastructure.[150] Additionally, in 2013, the Coast Guard created a Cyber Command to coordinate its cybersecurity efforts.[151]

The first goal of the strategy is the promotion of cyber risk awareness and management through risk assessment.[152] This goal has two objectives: 1) "Improve Port-Wide Cybersecurity Risk Assessment Tools and Methodologies," and 2) "Improve Cybersecurity Information Sharing."[153] To achieve these objectives, the Coast Guard will seek to leverage currently existing cybersecurity risk assessment tools, including those currently employed by the Coast Guard, and those employed by other agencies and industries.[154] It will also take steps to establish information sharing protocols and work with industry partners and other government agencies to facilitate information sharing across critical infrastructure sectors.[155]

---

[147] *See supra* Section III.
[148] U.S. COAST GUARD, *supra* note 19, at 5.
[149] *Id.* at 31.
[150] *Id.* at 32-33.
[151] *Id.* at 7.
[152] *Id.* at 32 ("The Coast Guard will incorporate cybersecurity into aspects of maritime operations in order to reduce the risk . . . and to continue to protect the nation's maritime critical infrastructure and the American people.").
[153] U.S. COAST GUARD, *supra* note 19, at 32.
[154] *Id.*
[155] *Id.*

The second goal is aimed at prevention and seeks to "Reduce Cybersecurity Vulnerabilities."[156] This goal also has two objectives: 1) "Reduce Cyber Vulnerability for Vessels and Facilities," and 2) "Incorporate Cybersecurity into Training and Education Requirements."[157] These objectives target development of guidance and education by working with industry partners, including international organizations, to determine best practices and protocols.[158]

C. Recent Cybersecurity Legislation

1. 2014 Cybersecurity Legislation

Prior to December 2014, no cybersecurity laws had been enacted since the Federal Information Security Management Act of 2002.[159] In December 2014, however, Congress approved five Acts related to cybersecurity.[160] The legislation most closely related to critical infrastructure and marine transportation are the National Cybersecurity Protection Act of 2014 and the Cybersecurity Enforcement Act of 2014.

---

[156] *Id.* at 33 ("Understanding the vulnerabilities associated with cyber systems enables the Coast Guard and the marine industry to take appropriate steps to reduce the risk to maritime cyber critical infrastructure from attack, exploitation, failure, or misuse.").
[157] *Id.*
[158] U.S. COAST GUARD, *supra* note 19, at 33.
[159] Lawrence J. Trautman, Article, *Cybersecurity: What About U.S. Policy?*, 2015 U. Ill. J.L. Tech. & Pol'y 341, 344 (2015).
[160] *Id.* (these include the National Cybersecurity Protection Act of 2014, the Federal Information Security Modernization Act of 2014, the Cybersecurity Workforce Assessment Act, the Homeland Security Workforce Assessment Act, and the Cybersecurity Enhancement Act of 2014).

a. National Cybersecurity Protection Act of 2014

The National Cybersecurity Protection Act of 2014 amends the Homeland Security Act of 2002, adding a provision for a National Cybersecurity and Communications Integration Center (NCCIC).[161] According to the Department of Homeland Security, NCCIC "is a 24x7 cyber situational awareness, incident response, and management center that is a national nexus of cyber and communications integration for the Federal Government, intelligence community, and law enforcement."[162] The mission of NCCIC is to decrease the severity and likelihood of events that may cause considerable compromise to the resilience and security of key national communications and information technology networks.[163]

A recent policy letter released by the Coast Guard regarding MTSA regulated facilities and vessels allows certain cyber incidents to be reported to the NCCIC.[164] The policy included cyber incidents in the definitions of reportable breaches of security and suspicious activity.[165] It was also noted that "[p]lausible terrorist attack scenarios include combined cyber and physical incidents."[166] Once a cyber incident is reported, "the NCCIC may be able to provide technical assistance to the porting party."[167]

In addition to establishing the NCCIC, the Cybersecurity Protection Act contains a number of provisions addressing information sharing and required reports.[168] Furthermore, for the critical infrastructure sector, it requires the DHS under Secretary for Critical Infrastructure Protection and Cybersecurity to "develop, regularly update, maintain, and exercise adaptable cyber incident response plans to address cybersecurity risks . . . to critical infrastructure."[169] These plans are to be developed in coordination with appropriate Federal, State, local, and industry partners.[170]

---

[161] Nat'l Cybersecurity Protection Act of 2014, Pub. L. No. 113-282, 128 Stat. 3066 (2014).
[162] *National Cybersecurity & Communications Integration Center*, U.S. DEP'T OF HOMELAND SECURITY, https://www.dhs.gov/national-cybersecurity-and-communications-integration-center (last visited Dec. 22, 2016).
[163] *Id.*
[164] U.S. Coast Guard, Policy Letter on Reporting Suspicious Activity & Breaches of Security (Dec. 14, 2016), https://homeport.uscg.mil (click on "Maritime Security" on the left menu bar and then "Policy." This letter is listed as "CG-5P Policy Ltr No. 08-16, Reporting Suspicious Activity & Breaches of Security") (Transportation Security Incidents are normally reported to the National Response Center. However, "cyber incidents that do not also involve physical or pollution effects" may now be reported "to the NCIC in lieu of the NRC . . . .").
[165] *Id.* at ¶ 3.A & B.
[166] *Id.* at ¶ 2.D.
[167] *Id.* at ¶ 3.C.iii.
[168] Nat'l Cybersecurity Protection Act of 2014, Pub. L. No. 113-282, 128 Stat. 3066 (2014).
[169] *Id.* at § 7.
[170] *Id.*

b. Cybersecurity Enhancement Act of 2014

The Cybersecurity Enhancement Act of 2014 is "An Act to provide for an ongoing, voluntary public-private partnership to improve cybersecurity, and to strengthen cybersecurity research and development, workforce development and education, and public awareness and preparedness, and for other purposes."[171] Title I of the Act amends the National Institute of Standards and Technology Act (15 U.S.C. 272), adding provisions that strengthen public-private collaboration in the cybersecurity realm, including "on an ongoing basis, facilitate and support the development of a voluntary, consensus-based, industry-led set of standards . . . to cost-effectively reduce cyber risks to critical infrastructure."[172]

Title II of the act focuses on cybersecurity research and development.[173] Among other provisions, it directs the development of a federal cybersecurity research and development strategic plan that is to be updated every four years and be "based on an assessment of cybersecurity risk to guide the overall direction of Federal cybersecurity and information assurance research and development . . . ."[174] While this strategic plan is to guide Federal cybersecurity research, in developing and updating the plan, the government entities are to work closely with the private sector, including academia, industry, and interested stakeholders.[175] This will allow the government to solicit recommendations and ensure that Federal research is not duplicating current private sector plans.[176]

Title III of the Act involves education and workforce development.[177] This portion of the Act promotes challenges and competitions to stimulate cybersecurity innovation and learning.[178] It also codifies a scholarship-for-service program designed to train and recruit promising individuals to fulfil cybersecurity positions at the tribal, local, State, and Federal levels.[179] Title IV, Cybersecurity Awareness and Preparedness, involves education.[180] Specifically, it orders the NIST Director, in consultation with other appropriate agencies and stakeholders, "to coordinate a national cybersecurity awareness and education program . . . ."[181]

Title V, Advancement of Cybersecurity Technical Standards, directs NIST to ensure coordination between agencies developing international technical information system security standards, to develop a cloud computing strategy for the Federal Government, and to support identity management research and development.[182] In the first two tasks, NIST is explicitly directed to consult with "other relevant Federal agencies and stakeholders from the private sector."[183]

---

[171] Cybersecurity Enhancement Act of 2014, Pub. L. No. 113-274, 128 Stat. 2971 (2014).
[172] *Id.* at § 101(a).
[173] *Id.* at § 201.
[174] *Id.* at § 201(a)(1).
[175] *Id.* at § 201(a)(2)(B).
[176] Cybersecurity Enhancement Act of 2014, Pub. L. No. 113-274, 128 Stat. 2971 § 201(a)(2)(B) (2014).
[177] *Id.* at §§ 301-302.
[178] *Id.* at § 301.
[179] *Id.* at § 302.
[180] *Id.* at § 401.
[181] Cybersecurity Enhancement Act of 2014, Pub. L. No. 113-274, 128 Stat. 2971 § 401(a). (2014).
[182] *Id.* at §§ 501-504.
[183] *Id.* at §§ 502-503.

2. Cybersecurity Act of 2015 and Recent Presidential Policy

Information sharing has been one of the most consistently contentious issues across the cyber domain.[184] Obstacles that have hindered information exchange include: the concerns that shared information could be used as evidence of failing to meet a regulatory standard, that after being shared with the government such information might be available to the public through a public records request, and concern over individual privacy rights.[185] The Cybersecurity Act of 2015 seeks to "facilitate and promote" timely information sharing across Federal and non-Federal entities to encourage sharing of information about cyber threats.[186]

a. Cybersecurity Act of 2015

The majority of the Cybersecurity Act is focused on information sharing.[187] It requires the Departments of Justice and Homeland Security to develop procedures to promote timely sharing of cyber information.[188] The Act also provides some key protections to private sector entities that share cybersecurity information.[189] It exempts information from disclosure via the Freedom of Information Act and requires that entities sharing information remove material that identifies specific individuals.[190] Additionally, the Act limits how federal, state, tribal, and local governments can use the information.[191] It specifically states that information "shared with a State, tribal, or local government . . . shall not be used . . . to regulate, including an enforcement action, the lawful activity of any non-Federal entity."[192] The federal government may only use the information for a limited number of purposes, including "a cybersecurity purpose,"[193] identifying cybersecurity vulnerabilities or threats, or a purpose related to other specified threats.[194] Additionally, the Act includes an entire section on "Protection from liability."[195] Legal commentators have suggested that such liability protection is a significant incentive to share information.[196] The Act specifically states that "[n]o cause of action shall lie or be maintained in any court against any private entity, and such action shall be promptly dismissed . . ." for information shared in accordance with the Act.[197]

---

[184] Peter Carey et al., *President Obama Signs Cybersecurity Act of 2015 to Encourage Cybersecurity Information Sharing*, NAT'L L. REV., (January 3, 2016).
[185] *Id.*
[186] 6 U.S.C.A. § 1502 (2015).
[187] Peter Carey et al., *supra* note 182.
[188] 6 U.S.C.A. § 1502 (2015).
[189] Peter Carey et al., *supra* note 182.
[190] 6 U.S.C.A. § 1503 (2015).
[191] 6 U.S.C.A. §§ 1503, 1504 (2015).
[192] 6 U.S.C.A. § 1503(4)(C) (2015).
[193] 6 U.S.C.A. § 1501 (2015) ("The term 'cybersecurity purpose' means the purpose of protecting an information system or information that is stored on, processed by, or transiting an information system from a cybersecurity threat or security vulnerability.").
[194] 6 U.S.C.A. § 1504(5)(A) (2015) (the other threats include death, serious bodily or economic harm, terrorist acts, "a serious threat to a minor," fraud or identify theft, espionage, or trade secret protection).
[195] 6 U.S.C.A. § 1505 (2015).
[196] Peter Carey et al, *supra* note 182.
[197] 6 U.S.C.A. § 1505(a), (b) (2015).

b. 2016 Presidential Policy

In February 2016, President Obama signed Executive Order 13718, creating a Commission on Enhancing National Cybersecurity under the Department of Commerce.[198] The Commission was made up of twelve members and included former government officials as well as representatives from academia and industry.[199] Executive Order 13718 directed the Commission to compile a report that included "detailed recommendations to strengthen cybersecurity in both the public and private sectors . . . ."[200]

The report was completed on December 1, 2016, and highlighted the critical need for partnerships between the private and public sectors.[201] The report identified six "major imperatives" which were further broken down into sixteen recommendations and fifty-three action items.[202] The Commission felt "that most recommendations can and should begin in the near term, with many meriting action within the first 100 days of the new Administration."[203] The aim of the report was to make recommendations for actions that can be incorporated during the next decade to help increase cybersecurity in both the private and public sectors.[204]

---

[198] Exec. Order No. 13718, 81 Fed. Reg. 29 (Feb. 9, 2016).
[199] *Comm'n on Enhancing Nat'l Cybersecurity*, NAT'L INST. OF STANDARDS & TECH., https://www.nist.gov/cybercommission (last visited Jan. 23, 2017).
[200] Exec. Order No. 13718, *supra* note 197 at § 3.
[201] COMM'N ON ENHANCING NAT'L CYBERSECURITY, REPORT ON SECURING AND GROWING THE DIGITAL ECONOMY (Dec. 1, 2016), https://www.nist.gov/sites/default/files/documents/2016/12/02/cybersecurity-commission-report-final-post.pdf.
[202] *Id.* at 2 ("The imperatives are: 1. Protect, defend, and secure today's information infrastructure and digital networks. 2. Innovate and accelerate investment for the security and growth of digital networks and the digital economy. 3. Prepare consumers to thrive in a digital age. 4. Build cybersecurity workforce capabilities. 5. Better equip government to function effectively and securely in the digital age. 6. Ensure an open, fair, competitive, and secure global digital economy.").
[203] *Id.*
[204] Exec. Order No. 13718, *supra* note 196, § 3. R4.1

The introduction to Presidential Policy Directive 41 (PPD-41), "United States Cyber Incident Coordination," notes that U.S. infrastructure "is vulnerable to malicious activity, malfunction, human error, and acts of nature, placing the Nation and its people at risk. Cyber incidents are a fact of contemporary life, and significant cyber incidents are occurring with increasing frequency . . . ."[205] PPD-41 highlights the shared responsibility of government, private sector, and individual stakeholders.[206] Further, it delineates principles under which the Federal Government are to respond to cyber incidents (involving either private sector or government entities).[207] For what the PPD termed "significant cyber incidents,"[208] lead Federal agencies were designated "and an architecture for coordinating the broader Federal Government response" was established.[209] PPD-41 mandated coordinated and "concurrent lines of effort" by federal agencies.[210] The "concurrent lines of effort" are divided into four areas of response, three undertaken for all cyber incidents, and the fourth only when a federal government agency is the affected party.[211] The first three areas are "threat response; asset response; and intelligence support and related activities."[212] The final response area is "to manage the effects of the cyber incident on [the affected federal agency's] operations, customers, and workforce."[213]

Threat response is focused on investigation, collecting evidence and intelligence, working to link related incidents, mitigation of any immediate threats, and other related tasks.[214] Another goal is to "facilitat[e] information sharing and operational coordination with asset response."[215] Asset response provides technical assistance to the parties affected by cyber incidents, to help them "protect their assets, mitigate vulnerabilities, and reduce impacts of cyber incidents . . . ."[216] Additionally, this area of response looks beyond the immediate threat vector to consider other entities and areas that may be vulnerable.[217] Asset responders also assist by "providing guidance on how best to utilize Federal resources and capabilities in a timely, effective manner to speed recovery."[218] The threat and asset response areas are designed to be closely related and enhance communications and information sharing.[219] The intelligence support activity focuses on building situational awareness, analyzing threats, identifying gaps, and gaining the ability to mitigate or degrade adversarial threat capabilities.[220]

---

[205] Presidential Policy Directive/PPD-41, *supra* note 73.
[206] *Id.*
[207] *Id.*
[208] *Id.* § II.B ("Significant cyber incident. A cyber incident that is (or group of related cyber incidents that together are) likely to result in demonstrable harm to the national security interests, foreign relations, or economy of the United States or to the public confidence, civil liberties, or public health and safety of the American people.").
[209] Presidential Policy Directive/PPD-41 § I, *supra* note 73.
[210] *Id.* § IV.
[211] Presidential Policy Directive/PPD-41, *supra* note 73, § IV.
[212] *Id.*
[213] *Id.*
[214] *Id.* § IV.A.
[215] Presidential Policy Directive/PPD-41, *supra* note 73, § IV.B.
[216] *Id.*
[217] *Id.*
[218] *Id.*
[219] *Id.*
[220] *Id.* at § IV.C. R4.1.

When a federal agency is an affected party, efforts will be taken to manage the effects of the incident.[221] This "line of effort" will be managed by the affected agency and will include broad-ranging efforts, from external affairs to ensuring operational continuity.[222] When a private entity is the affected party, the government will not play an active role in managing the effects of the incident, "but it will remain cognizant of the affected entity's response activities . . . ."[223] For private sector entities, the most relevant government agency will generally be responsible for maintaining this awareness.[224]

Given the shared responsibility held by both the government and private sector, it is also important for the private sector to cultivate situational awareness and develop threat response procedures. Developing industry guidelines and procedures is an effective way to share best practices and lessons learned. Such guidelines should be shared across company lines and with the government so that all industry partners can benefit from the information.

---

[221] Presidential Policy Directive/PPD-41, *supra* note 73, § IV.D.
[222] *Id.*
[223] *Id.*
[224] *Id.*

III. Maritime Industry Practice and Guidance

The maritime industry has recently taken an increased notice of cyber risk. Three industry-leading organizations promulgated guidance in 2016 alone. These guidelines and suggestions highlight best practices and approaches to address maritime cyber risk management. While differing in scope, some basic principles emerge that are consistent throughout the guidelines. All three advocate integrating the NIST Framework principles into the industry's cyber approaches. Additionally, increasing cyber awareness was recognized as a critical step in improving cybersecurity. While the American Bureau of Shipping Guidance Notes are by far the most thorough, each of the industry guidelines bring an important perspective to the table. These guidelines are important, not so much for the techniques and procedures they discuss, but for the fact that these highly influential maritime organizations are taking notice of the cyber threat and working to increase industry awareness.

A. *Baltic and International Maritime Council: The Guidelines on Cyber Security Onboard Ships*

"The Guidelines on Cyber Security Onboard Ships," released by the Baltic and International Maritime Council (BIMCO) and several other influential maritime associations, is tailored to ship-owners and operators.[225] The Guidelines are designed to give pointers on assessing operations and implementing the necessary actions and procedures to maintain cybersecurity aboard ships.[226] The "Guidelines focus on the unique issues facing the shipping industry onboard ships."[227] Additionally, the Guidelines aim to improve awareness and understanding of good cybersecurity practices.[228]

---

[225] Baltic & Int'l Mar. Council, The Guidelines on Cyber Security Onboard Ships 1 (Version 1.1, 2016), https://www.marad.dot.gov/wp-content/uploads/pdf/Guidelines_on_cyber_security_onboard_ships_version_1-1_Feb2016.pdf.
[226] *Id.*
[227] *Id.*
[228] *Id.*

The Guidelines set out a framework for cybersecurity awareness that includes six related steps: identify threats; identify vulnerabilities; assess risk exposure; develop protection and detection measures; establish contingency plans; and respond to cyber security incidents.[229] To identify threats, a ship owner or operator must understand both the external and internal[230] threat possibilities.[231] While cyber risk is pervasive, each maritime entity needs to identify the specific risks to their operation, company, trade, or vessel.[232] In identifying vulnerabilities, companies need to cultivate awareness "of any specific aspect of their operations that might increase their vulnerability to cyber incidents."[233] Additionally, the Guidelines point out that each entity must have knowledge and understanding of any protection measures already in place and the capabilities and limitations of these measures.[234]

In assessing risk exposure, the Guidelines specify that any cyber protections already in place, along with the specific vulnerabilities that are found in the maritime industry, should be considered.[235] The maritime realm presents a number of features that are potentially vulnerable to cyber threats. "Multiple stakeholders are often involved in the operation and chartering of a ship potentially resulting in lack of accountability for the IT infrastructure."[236] Additionally, ships regularly "interface[] with other parts of the global supply chain . . . [and share information] with shore-based service providers."[237] Furthermore, many ship systems, including those related to environmental protection and safety, are controlled by computers.[238] The Guidelines suggest using the NIST framework to assess current approaches and help identify risks.[239] It is additionally suggested that each company should conduct an internal risk assessment to identify potential threats and survey current systems and procedures.[240] This self-assessment should be followed up by a third-party assessment to find any additional threat vectors missed during the self-assessment.[241]

---

[229] *Id.* at 2.
[230] *Id.*
[231] BALTIC & INT'L MAR. COUNCIL, THE GUIDELINES ON CYBER SECURITY ONBOARD SHIPS 1 (Version 1.1, 2016), https://www.marad.dot.gov/wp-content/uploads/pdf/Guidelines_on_cyber_security_onboard_ships_version_1-1_Feb2016.pdf. (Internal threat possibilities are caused by insufficient awareness or inappropriate use).
[232] *Id.* at 3.
[233] *Id.*
[234] *Id.* at 2.
[235] *Id.* at 6.
[236] *Id.*
[237] BALTIC & INT'L MAR. COUNCIL, THE GUIDELINES ON CYBER SECURITY ONBOARD SHIPS 1 (Version 1.1, 2016), https://www.marad.dot.gov/wp-content/uploads/pdf/Guidelines_on_cyber_security_onboard_ships_version_1-1_Feb2016.pdf. at 6.
[238] *Id.*
[239] *Id.*
[240] *Id.* at 7.
[241] *Id.* at 10.

Reducing risk through the development of protection and detection measures is one of the most important steps in the cybersecurity awareness cycle. The Guidelines suggest implementing a layered approach that focuses on both technical and procedural defenses.[242] Technical defenses are "focused on ensuring that onboard systems are designed and configured to be resilient to cyber-attacks."[243] Procedural defenses ensure that company policies, procedures (both safety and security), and access controls cover cyber vulnerabilities.[244] One critical procedural control identified by the Guidelines is ensuring adequate training and awareness of personnel who operate and support the ship.[245]

Each company should establish "appropriate contingency plans in order to effectively respond to cyber incidents."[246] These plans should be periodically tested so that personnel are familiar with the appropriate procedures to follow in the case of a cyber incident.[247] The Guidelines further suggest that these plans should be available in some type of non-electronic form in case the cyber incident involves deleting or disrupting access to data.[248]

According to the Guidelines, the final step, "respond to cyber security incidents," should be informed by all the previous steps in the awareness cycle.[249] Furthermore, the plans that were developed should be implemented, and their effectiveness measured.[250] The Guidelines also specify that vulnerabilities and threats should be re-evaluated in light of the actual incident.[251]

---

[242] *Id.* at 12.
[243] BALTIC & INT'L MAR. COUNCIL, THE GUIDELINES ON CYBER SECURITY ONBOARD SHIPS 1 (Version 1.1, 2016), https://www.marad.dot.gov/wp-content/uploads/pdf/Guidelines_on_cyber_security_onboard_ships_version_1-1_Feb2016.pdf.
[244] *Id.*
[245] *Id.* at 15.
[246] *Id.* at 18.
[247] *Id.*
[248] *Id.*
[249] BALTIC & INT'L MAR. COUNCIL, THE GUIDELINES ON CYBER SECURITY ONBOARD SHIPS 1 (Version 1.1, 2016), https://www.marad.dot.gov/wp-content/uploads/pdf/Guidelines_on_cyber_security_onboard_ships_version_1-1_Feb2016.pdf.
[250] *Id.*
[251] *Id.*

B. *International Maritime Organization: Interim Guidelines on Maritime Cyber Risk Management*

The Maritime Safety Committee of the International Maritime Organization (IMO) approved and published "Interim Guidelines on Maritime Cyber Risk Management" in June 2016.[252] The Committee's reason for releasing the Guidelines was "the urgent need to raise awareness on cyber risk threats and vulnerabilities."[253] This short document gives a broad overview of items to consider related to cyber risk and references both the NIST Framework and the BIMCO Guidelines.[254] The IMO Guidelines focus on a risk management approach and are designed to be incorporated with existing industry processes and procedures.[255]

The Guidelines advocate creating a culture of cyber risk awareness that starts at the most senior level of management and flows throughout every level of an organization.[256] In order to create and sustain this culture of risk awareness, the Guidelines focus on the same five functional elements identified in the NIST framework: identify, protect, detect, respond, and recover.[257] The Guidelines note that the "functional elements are not sequential—all should be concurrent and continuous in practice and should be incorporated appropriately in a risk management framework."[258]

The "identify" element contains a suggestion that all personnel responsibilities and roles related to cybersecurity should be identified.[259] Additionally, any critical data, capabilities, assets or systems that are potential vulnerable to cyber-attack should also be identified.[260] Under "protect," IMO advocates implementing risk control measures and processes that focus on protecting against a potential cyber event, and aim to ensure operational continuity in the face of such an event.[261] The "detect," "respond," and "recover" elements focus on developing and implementing processes that effectively allow organizations to detect a cyber event, and respond in such a way that allows for timely restoral and recovery of critical systems.[262]

---

[252] INT'L MAR. ORG., INTERIM GUIDELINES ON MARITIME CYBER RISK MANAGEMENT, MSC.1/CIRC. 1526 (2016), https://www.marad.dot.gov/wp-content/uploads/pdf/MSC.1-Circ.1526-Interim-Guidelines-On-Maritime-Cyber-Risk-Management-....pdf.
[253] *Id.*
[254] *Id.* at 4.
[255] *Id.* at 1.
[256] *Id.* at 3.
[257] *Id.*
[258] INT'L MAR. ORG., *supra* note 250 at 3.
[259] *Id.*
[260] *Id.*
[261] *Id.*
[262] *Id.*

C. American Bureau of Shipping CyberSafety™ Guidance Notes

In 2016, the American Bureau of Shipping (ABS)[263] released a series of five volumes of CyberSafety™ Guidance Notes. This series is by far the most detailed guidance available for maritime cybersecurity. In the Foreword to the second volume of the series, ABS notes that "[e]xposure to these [cyber] threats has become pervasive due to the exponential growth of automation methods—and increasingly, autonomy—that has penetrated nearly all aspects of shipboard and offshore asset systems."[264] ABS points out that since such systems are integral to multiple facets of platform, ship, or asset operations, they are critical to operational safety and security.[265]

Volume 1: *Cybersecurity*, published in February 2016, offers cybersecurity commentary and best practices.[266] Cyber awareness should be "a foundational element of overall safety and security within and across the marine and offshore communities."[267] The volume is divided into five sections. The first two sections are more general in nature, discussing cybersecurity and giving advice on developing a cybersecurity program. The last three sections gather best practices that apply to marine and offshore operations. In discussing best practices, ABS advocates have developed nine basic capabilities as the foundation of a successful cybersecurity program.[268] Once the baseline capabilities are established, additional capabilities should be developed to provide increasing breadth and depth to a cybersecurity program.[269]

---

[263] ABS is an internationally recognized classification society. A classification society is "an organization that develops official standards for the shipping industry and checks the condition of ships and their equipment to make certain they are safe and meet the official standards of the shipping industry." *Classification Society*, CAMBRIDGE BUSINESS ENGLISH DICTIONARY, http://dictionary.cambridge.org/us/dictionary/english/classification-society (last visited Mar. 28, 2017).
[264] American Bureau of Shipping, *Guide for: Cybersecurity Implementation for the Marine and Offshore Industries*, 2 ABS CYBERSAFETY™ ii (2016), http://ww2.eagle.org/content/dam/eagle/rules-and-guides/current/other/251_cybersafetyV2/CyberSafety_V2_Cybersecurity_Guide_e.pdf.
[265] *Id.*
[266] American Bureau of Shipping, *Guidance Notes on: the Application of Cybersecurity Principles to Marine And Offshore Operations*, 1 ABS CYBERSAFETY™ ii (2016), http://ww2.eagle.org/content/dam/eagle/rules-and-guides/current/other/250_cybersafetyV1/CyberSafety_V1_Cybersecurity_GN_e.pdf.
[267] *Id.* at ii.
[268] *Id.* at Fig. 1 (the basic capabilities are: "1-Exercise Best Practices; 2-Build the Security Organization; 3-Provision for Employee Awareness & Training; 4-Perform Risk Assessment; 5-Provide Perimeter Defense; 6-Prepare for Incident Response & Recovery; 7-Provide Physical Security; 8-Execute Access Management; and 9-Maintain Asset Management").
[269] *Id.* at 5.

Volume 2, published in September 2016,[270] establishes criteria to assess the readiness of assets and systems to prevent cyber incidents that could compromise the security and/or safety of assets, systems, and critical data.[271] This volume, referred to as a Guide, "provides a model for implementing cybersecurity programs."[272] A ship under the classification purview of ABS that complies with the criteria and procedures identified in the Guide can be issued a "CyberSafety Management System Certificate (CMSC) and Notation . . . ."[273] Additionally, a facility can be issued a "Certificate of Cyber Compliance (CCC)."[274] The Guide lays out detailed procedures and processes for obtaining and maintaining certification.[275]

Volume 3 is specifically focused on "data integrity."[276] This particular Guidance Note "is intended to help the industry realize the new benefits from data sources and data analytics systems via implementation of Data Integrity concepts."[277] The Note focuses on three main areas: characterizing data, securing data, and maintaining data integrity.[278]

---

[270] Volumes 2–5 were all published in September 2016.
[271] *See* American Bureau of Shipping, *supra* note 263 at ii.
[272] *Id.* at 1.
[273] *Id.* (Vessels or "offshore assets not classed by ABS can be issued a 'Statement of Fact' when they are in conformance with the requirements of this Guide.").
[274] *Id.*
[275] *Id.* at 2–4.
[276] American Bureau of Shipping, *Guidance Notes on: Data Integrity for Marine and Offshore Operations*, 3 ABS CYBERSAFETY™ ii (2016), http://ww2.eagle.org/content/dam/eagle/rules-and-guides/current/other/252_cybersafetyV3/CyberSafety_V3_Data_Integrity_GN_e.pdf.
[277] *Id.*
[278] *Id.* at 3.

Volume 4, the *Guide for Software Systems Verification*, is focused on the software component of the control systems found onboard vessels (and offshore assets).[279] "The objective of this Guide is to reduce software-related incidents that could negatively affect the security, safety and performance of [computer-based control] systems."[280] The Guide presents various criteria and processes designed to verify the software portion of vessel control systems.[281] ABS suggests that the "verification and validation organization" (used to perform software verification) should be a completely independent third-party.[282] Systems identified as of particular note include dynamic positioning, power management, thruster control, and blowout prevention.[283] This Guide focuses exclusively on software and does not provide procedures to verify hardware.[284] A vessel that conforms to the criteria and procedures outlined in the Guide may be granted an "SSV" notation to indicate compliance.[285]

Volume 5 is designed to augment ABS's *Guide for Integrated Software Quality Management (ISQM)*.[286] The *ISQM* "presents a risk-based software development and maintenance process . . . based upon internationally recognized standards."[287] This volume is designed mainly for software system providers involved in software design and quality assurance.[288]

---

[279] American Bureau of Shipping, *Guide for: Software Systems Verification*, 4 ABS CYBERSAFETY™ ii (2016), http://ww2.eagle.org/content/dam/eagle/rules-and-guides/current/other/253_cybersafetyV4/CyberSafety_V4_SSV_Guide_e.pdf.
[280] *Id.* at 1.
[281] *Id.* at 6.
[282] *Id.* at 3. *Id.* at 3. A Verification and Validation Organization (V&V) is "[t]he organization that develops the verification plan and performs the software verification of the control system." The V&V must be an independent third party unless "special consideration" is requested from ABS and ABS determines that "sufficient independence" exists between the V&V and the system provider of the software being verified.
[283] *Id.* at 13–14; Occupational Safety & Health Admin., *Oil and Gas Well Drilling and Servicing eTool: Drilling—Blowout Preventers*, U.S. DEP'T OF LABOR, https://www.osha.gov/SLTC/etools/oilandgas/drilling/wellcontrol_bop.html (last visited Feb. 11, 2017) (a blowout preventer is designed to prevent blowout from occurring on an oil or gas well by "shut[ting] off the well hole and prevent[ing] the escape of the underground fluids").
[284] 4 AMERICAN BUREAU OF SHIPPING, *supra* note 278 at 8.
[285] *Id.* at 1.
[286] 5 AMERICAN BUREAU OF SHIPPING, ABS CYBERSAFETY™ GUIDANCE NOTES ON SOFTWARE PROVIDER CONFORMITY PROGRAM ii (2016), http://ww2.eagle.org/content/dam/eagle/rules-and-guides/current/other/254_cybersafetyV5/CyberSafety_V5_SPCP_GN_e.pdf.
[287] *Id.*
[288] *Id.* at 1.

The ABS standards are by far the most detailed and thorough currently available in the maritime domain. ABS, as a classification society, carries great weight in the maritime industry. "In the absence of classification societies for ships, there would be no benchmark or guideline standards for vessels and other constructions to adhere to."[289] Thus, the ABS CyberSafety™ Guidance Notes are a big step forward for the cybersecurity practices of the maritime industry and should be used as a template for future industry tactics, techniques, and procedures. Wide adoption of the ABS standards and creation of similar standards by other classification societies will allow the maritime industry to vastly improve cybersecurity awareness and preparation, effectively reducing cyber vulnerabilities.

IV. RECOMMENDATIONS

Recently the U.S. government and the maritime industry have made good strides towards addressing cybersecurity issues in the maritime domain. However, while a good foundation currently exists, the industry and government need to continue to build on that foundation. The next steps include creating a pervasive culture of cyber risk awareness, ensuring that to the extent possible, MTSA required security plans address cyber risk, and revising current regulations or developing new regulations to focus on cybersecurity.

A. *Create a Culture of Cyber Risk Awareness*

All components of the marine transportation sector—government, port facilities, ship owners and operators, and other related entities—need to create a culture of cyber risk awareness. This culture needs to be supported by the highest levels of management and continue down through all personnel who access systems vulnerable to cyber-attack. Indeed, the BIMCO Guidelines specifically state that "[c]yber security should start at the senior management level of a company . . . ."[290] The key to implementing such a culture is educating personnel on cyber vulnerabilities and types of threats. All of the materials reviewed for this Note advocated the creation of a total organizational culture that promoted cyber risk awareness. Until this type of culture is in place, and robust cyber awareness training and education is the norm, each organization is only as safe as its least educated employee with access to critical systems.

B. *Ensure MTSA Required Plans Address Cyber Risk*

The requirements promulgated under MTSA for area maritime, facility, and vessel security plans can be considered to include cyber elements through the communications and security systems section.[291] In creating, updating, and evaluating vessel and facility security plans, emphasis should be placed on ensuring that cyber vulnerabilities are considered and addressed. The Coast Guard and AMS Committees should make addressing cyber risk a top priority.

---

[289] Sharda, *The Importance of Classification Societies in the Maritime Industry*, MARINE INSIGHT (July 21, 2016), http://www.marineinsight.com/maritime-law/the-importance-of-classification-societies-in-the-maritime-industry/.
[290] BALTIC & INT'L MAR. COUNCIL, *supra* note 249 at 6.
[291] 33 C.F.R. §§ 103.405, 104.405, 105.405 (2016).

The NIST Framework is a useful tool for companies and organizations to use in evaluating current approaches to cybersecurity. The Coast Guard, AMS Committees, classification societies, and maritime organizations should encourage use of the Framework when addressing cyber risk. The procedures put in place based on NIST Tiers and Profiles should be included in all MTSA required plans.

Once MTSA required plans include cyber elements, the planned response to cyber-attacks should be regularly tested through drills and exercises. This will help ensure that employees and regulators are familiar with the policies and procedures set forth in the plans. It will also help identify any gaps in the plans. Identifying gaps in an environment where the risk is simulated and failure does not cause irreparable damage is preferable to discovering gaps during an actual attack. Furthermore, it will allow individuals who have been identified in the plans as having decision-making authority to practice making decisions related to cyber-attacks.

The Port Security Grant Program (PSGP) should continue to emphasize cybersecurity as a critical priority. This funding opportunity can assist maritime companies and port stakeholders in paying for third-party assessments, or gaining equipment needed to close cyber vulnerabilities identified in such assessments.[292] However, FEMA should ensure appropriate standards are promulgated for review of cyber projects under the PSGP. These standards should include provisions to allow both field and national level reviewers to consult with appropriate cyber experts during the review process.

C. *Develop Additional Maritime Focused Cybersecurity Legislation*

While MTSA can be read to include cyber, it would be better to either pass legislation that amended MTSA to explicitly include cybersecurity, or create new legislation specifically focused on cybersecurity in the maritime sector. Legislation designed to revise and amend MTSA would clearly signal that cyber threats and vulnerabilities are an important part of the security of United States seaports and vessels. Even MTSA was an amendment to an earlier act (the Merchant Marine Act of 1936).[293] Any revision of MTSA should update the definition of a transportation security incident to clearly include cyber-related disruptions.[294] Additionally, any revision of MTSA (or new legislation) should include a requirement for vessels and facilities to create, test, and maintain plans to address cybersecurity vulnerabilities and responses to cyber-attacks.

---

[292] *See e.g. DHS Needs to Enhance Efforts to Address Port Cybersecurity*, supra note 92 at 9.
[293] Maritime Transportation Security Act of 2002, Pub. L. No. 107-295, 116 Stat. 2064 (2002).
[294] *See* U.S. Coast Guard, *supra* note 163.

2014 and 2015 saw a significant increase in cybersecurity legislation.[295] However, many additional governmental cybersecurity polices were promulgated by Executive Order and Presidential Policy Directive. With a major change in administration occurring in January 2016, it is unknown how many of these policies and procedures will remain in effect or what focus the new administration will have on cybersecurity.[296] This uncertainty highlights the need for the creation of additional, durable cybersecurity legislation. The policies enacted through Executive Order and Presidential Policy Directive should be considered for inclusion in new or revised legislation. This way, the best and most effective of the practices identified in these presidential orders can be codified into legislation. This will allow such policies to endure even in the face of presidential transition.

V. Conclusion

Modern ships, facilities, and ports rely on integrated systems that are vulnerable to cyber-attacks. Thankfully, a major cyber-attack on the marine transportation sector has not yet occurred. However, significant manmade disruptions have shown the far-reaching effects such events could have on the prosperity and security of the United States.[297] The capabilities of cyber-terrorists are continuing to grow and develop, presenting increased risks to the industrial control systems employed by the maritime industry. Both the maritime industry and the federal government have begun to address the cyber threat in the maritime domain. However, both the industry and government need to continue building on this foundation and harden marine transportation against cyber threats. It is critical for all maritime partners to implement a culture of cyber risk awareness. This culture must be pervasive, reaching from the highest levels of management to the workers at the most junior levels. Additionally, the government should work with industry to share information, leverage current regulations to their full extent, and create new regulations that specifically focus on cybersecurity. Only through continuous vigilance and a willingness to share information will the marine transportation sector be able to protect its critical intellectual property and keep ports, facilities, and vessels safe from cyber threats.

---

[295] *See supra* Part II.C. Prior to 2014 no significant cybersecurity legislation had been enacted since 2002, however, in 2014 five Acts were approved and another major Act was passed in 2015.
[296] Joseph J. Lazzarotti, *President Donald J. Trump—What Lies Ahead for Privacy, Cybersecurity, e-Communication?*, 11/9/16 Nat'l L. Rev., 2016 WLNR 34340881 (2016).
[297] *See supra* Part I.A.